D1521843

The African-American Experience in the Civilian Conservation Corps

The African-American Experience

in the

CIVILIAN

CONSERVATION

CORPS

Olen Cole, Jr.

University Press of Florida

Gainesville · Tallahassee · Tampa · Boca Raton
Pensacola · Orlando · Miami · Jacksonville

333.76
C68a

Copyright 1999 by the Board of Regents of the State of Florida
Printed in the United States of America on acid-free paper
All rights reserved
All photographs courtesy of Donald Hobart

04 03 02 01 00 99 6 5 4 3 2 1

Library of Congress Cataloging-in-Publication Data
Cole, Olen, 1946–
The African-American experience in the
Civilian Conservation Corps / Olen Cole, Jr.
p. cm.
Includes bibliographical references and index.
ISBN 0-8130-1660-6 (alk. paper)
1. Civilian Conservation Corps (U.S.)—California—History.
2. Afro-American young men—Employment—California—History.
3. Afro-American young men—Education—California—History.
I. Title.
S932.C65   1999
333.76'16'08996073—dc21   98-43058

Cau

The University Press of Florida is the scholarly publishing agency
for the State University System of Florida, comprising Florida
A & M University, Florida Atlantic University, Florida International
University, Florida State University, University of Central Florida,
University of Florida, University of North Florida, University of
South Florida, and University of West Florida.

University Press of Florida
15 Northwest 15th Street
Gainesville, FL 32611–2079
http://www.upf.com

To my parents

University Libraries
Carnegie Mellon University
h. PA 15213-3890

CONTENTS

FIGURES AND TABLES

Illustrations

Tables, Charts, and Maps

PREFACE

The Great Depression of the 1930s created enormous hardship for many Americans, but the problems were especially acute for African-Americans. *The African-American Experience in the Civilian Conservation Corps* examines the participation of black youth in the Civilian Conservation Corps (CCC), one of the most successful New Deal agencies of President Franklin D. Roosevelt. This book assesses the operations of the CCC with regard to African-Americans' experiences in California and examines the manner in which African-American CCC workers were affected by the Corps and the actual contributions they made as participants.

The varied and distinctive experiences of the participants are revealed in their own stories through oral interviews. In chapter 1, former Corps members discuss the benefits they gained as a result of their experiences through employment and vocational training. Other chapters address topics such as community resistance to all-black CCC camps, educational and recreational programs, efforts to overcome racism, special work projects that made major contributions to the development, protection, and maintenance of California's national forest and parks, and the long-term impact of the CCC experience on African-American corpsmen in California.

With few exceptions, historians of the New Deal era have published far too little on African-Americans and the CCC, particularly at the state level. This book provides an opportunity for students interested in the New Deal, the West, and especially the experience of African-Americans in the twentieth century to explore a different approach to their encounter with the Civilian Conservation Corps.

A limited and slightly altered portion of this study appeared in an article for *Forest & Conservation History*. The complete citation is included in the bibliography. Whatever merit this study possesses derives in large measure from the advice, guidance, and suggestions provided by Professor Otis L.

Graham, Jr., my dissertation chairman at the University of North Carolina at Chapel Hill. With patience and understanding he provided thoughtful criticism and knowledge of the New Deal that helped to give this study a broader perspective than I could possibly have provided alone. To Professors R. Don Higginbotham, Nell I. Painter, George B. Tindall, and Lillie Edwards, members of my dissertation committee who provided the encouragement crucial to any student, I extend appreciation. I would also like to single out for special appreciation Professor Harold T. Pinkett, who first introduced the idea of a study of the African-American experience in the CCC. I owe a considerable debt to Donald Hobart, who provided photographs and CCC newspapers as well as his personal recollections of the Corps in California. To the former CCC enrollees and their families who graciously took the time to discuss their experiences in the Corps, I extend a special thanks. I would also like to extend my appreciation to the staffs of the National Archives, the Franklin D. Roosevelt Library, the Bancroft Library of the University of California at Berkeley, the California State Library, and the Manuscripts Department at the Library of Congress.

Special thanks are due the staff of the University Press of Florida and especially my editor, Meredith Morris-Babb, whose faith in this project will never be forgotten.

Finally, my family. Unquestionably, this endeavor would not have been completed without their love and support. To my wife, Phyllis Cole, who tirelessly read several drafts of the manuscript and whose encouragement remained solid, I am particularly grateful.

PROLOGUE

Growing up in America in the 1930s was not easy. The country was experiencing the worst economic depression in its history. It was almost impossible for young people—and especially difficult for young African-American men who were living in the South, where racial discrimination was practiced openly and often—to find employment.

Claude Ferguson Pierce was born and raised in rural Lincoln Parish, Louisiana, which is in the northern part of the state, about sixty miles north of Monroe, Louisiana. Claude was no stranger to poverty, and being one of fifteen in the Pierce household made times especially difficult for him and his family. The Great Depression had struck Lincoln Parish with devastating effect.

After completing high school in the spring of 1937 and having tried, unsuccessfully, to gain employment, Claude hopped a freight train for California. It was not uncommon at that time for thousands of teenagers in search of employment to use this mode of transportation. Claude met hundreds of transients like himself on the trains between Louisiana and California, all in search of work. Many of the African-American travelers indicated that they wanted to get away from the hard-core poverty of the South and its pervasive racism.

Upon his arrival in Los Angeles in the summer of 1937, Claude soon came to realize that the Golden State was experiencing hard times and, as in Louisiana, the African-American community was especially hard hit by the Depression. He applied for a job at a rug factory, stating his age as twenty-one, but when asked for proof, he had none. The foreman indicated that although he knew Claude would probably do a good job, he simply could not hire him because he suspected he was underage. The company could not afford the liability if Claude were injured.

Eventually Claude found employment with a prominent white family and worked for several weeks as a handyman. Then in August 1937, he signed up for the Civilian Conservation Corps (CCC). Shortly afterward, he received a letter of acceptance and was instructed to report to the CCC Reception Center in Van Nuys, California.

The two years that Claude Pierce served in the CCC would be perhaps the most memorable of his life. This book tells the story of that experience for Claude as well as for many others who chose the CCC as a way of life in the 1930s.

Introduction

The Civilian Conservation Corps is considered one of the most successful and popular of President Franklin D. Roosevelt's New Deal agencies. To assess the success of the CCC in California, I conducted a study to examine the manner in which African-American youth were affected by the CCC and the actual contributions made as participants. The study was based upon primary source materials from the National Archives, the Franklin D. Roosevelt Library, and records of the CCC within the state, as well as correspondence and interviews with former enrollees. I have concluded that, while historians and Americans in general have accepted the positive effects of the CCC experience on enrollees, no irrefutable evidence exists to confirm those effects, at least not on a long-term basis.

In California, the CCC's achievements are unquestionable. Not only did it provide jobs for unemployed youth, but it also contributed immensely to the state's conservation efforts as well. In the case of African-American corpsmen in California, the available evidence indicated that though essentially successful, the CCC had its share of problems. The legislation providing for the CCC stipulated that there should be no discrimination on the basis of race, color, or creed. The concept was ideal but the problems created by and for the African-American population were real. African-American corpsmen, when admitted, faced segregation, discrimination, and hostility both within the CCC program and from nearby white communities.

Yet the CCC in California temporarily provided some useful and important benefits for African-American enrollees. Indeed, the CCC presents an example of what can be accomplished when the federal government commits itself, if only for a brief period, to fulfill its obligations to all Americans, regardless of race, creed, or color.

Although the Great Depression of the 1930s affected all Americans, it struck some groups harder than others. Because of competition for jobs from a large number of jobless workers, those without experience or a specific skill found it extremely difficult, sometimes even impossible, to find employment. Among the groups particularly hard hit were America's young people. President Franklin D. Roosevelt responded to this effect of the Depression in March 1933 by creating the Civilian Conservation Corps. The CCC, aimed at the worst aspects of youth joblessness, bore Roosevelt's personal stamp of approval and support. The president's close support of the CCC expressed not only his firm belief that a rural environment offered the "best of all worlds" but reflected as well his concern for the conservation of America's enormous, though dwindling, supply of natural resources.

The origin of the CCC idea had its roots in Roosevelt's early childhood. As a child, Roosevelt developed an appreciation for nature, and he spent many hours exploring the hills and forests of his parents' estate at Hyde Park, New York. Early on, his father instilled in him a love for nature, especially trees, and FDR would in later years "demonstrate his love for his trees at Hyde Park by painting his favorites," which were the English oaks that stood near the entrance to what is today the Franklin D. Roosevelt Library. Arthur Schlesinger, Jr., has written that for a time FDR "planted twenty to fifty thousand trees a year on the estate."[1]

As governor of New York State, Roosevelt's interest in forests and conservation was carried into action on a statewide basis. In 1931, Governor Roosevelt gave his support to an amendment to the state constitution that would provide for the purchase of over one million acres of abandoned farmland suitable for reforestation. The amendment was adopted with a 200,000 vote majority. A year later, 10,345 men were employed by the New York State Conservation Department in reforestation of land and insect control.[2]

The new governor also believed that a rural existence "was the best of all possible worlds." His dream, according to Frank Friedel, was that city workers could be moved back to the land, "where they could raise some of their own produce. This was partly the Governor's sustained enthusiasm for his Uncle Ted's 'Country Life' movement, and partly Roosevelt's romantic faith in the Jeffersonian ideal of the independent yeoman living in bucolic abundance." In an August 1931 speech to the American Country Life Conference at Ithaca, New York, the governor elaborated: "There is contact with earth and with nature and the restful privilege of getting away from pavements and from noise. There is an opportunity for permanency of abode, a chance to establish a real home in the traditional American sense."[3]

At the national level, because of the necessity to put extreme emergency measures in place, some program would have to be established under strict limitations. There was no precedent for such a large undertaking as the CCC. Therefore, it would be important to proceed boldly, but carefully, instituting segments that had already been tried and proven to be successful, for example, the conservation measures used in Roosevelt's New York State efforts.

Indeed, the governor's interest in conservation would be consistent with his emphasis on the need for "planning" and "experimentation." In a speech to Oglethorpe University in April 1932, Roosevelt declared: "The country needs and, unless I mistake its temper, the country demands bold, persistent experimentation."[4] Roosevelt's commitment to conservation and his determination to help alleviate the problem of unemployment would continue when he became president of the United States.

In his message to Congress on March 21, 1933, the president declared: "I propose to create a civilian conservation corps to be used in simple work, not interfering with normal employment, and confining itself to forestry, the prevention of soil erosion, flood control and similar projects. I call your attention to the fact that this type of work is of definite practical value, not only through the prevention of great present financial loss but also as a means of creating future national wealth."[5] The president also proposed to employ men on public and private lands for the prevention of forest fires, plant pest and disease control, and the construction, maintenance, or repair of paths, trails, and fire lanes.

The Emergency Conservation Work (ECW) Act was passed by both houses of Congress, and on March 31, 1933, the president signed into law the Civilian Conservation Corps.[6] In general, the act enjoyed bipartisan support. Some opponents, however, labeled it "fascist," while others argued that the act would lead to "socialism." Members of Congress from the western section of the nation objected to the act, fearing that senators and congressmen from eastern urban areas "would use the CCC as a means of unloading this undesirable element and shipping them west."[7] However, with the persistence and political skill of Senator David Walsh of Massachusetts, the act was accepted in both houses of Congress and the Civilian Conservation Corps became mandated by law.[8]

While the subject of the CCC and the participation of African-Americans is at least acknowledged in most histories of the New Deal, and John A. Salmond has researched the agency's policy toward African-Americans nationally, little has been written on the African-American experience in the Corps at camp level, particularly in the West. In fact, one study has suggested that African-Americans and other minorities played such a nebulous and minor role in the Ninth Corps area (Montana, Idaho, Utah, Wyoming, Nevada, California, Oregon, and Washington) that their impact hardly warrants scholarly attention.[9]

Yet, however minor the role of African-Americans in the Ninth Corps area states, they were represented. In Montana, for instance, there was one African-American company located near Belton in 1933 and 1934. The white merchants of Belton, after hearing that an African-American company would be stationed near the town, placed cards in their windows that read: "We cater to white trade only." Wyoming had twelve African-American corpsmen in 1933, all of whom were assigned to Camps Guernsey and Chimney Park. In May 1938, the white citizens of Rawlins, Wyoming, upon receiving word that an African-American company from Texas was being sent to a CCC camp nearby, protested that African-American enrollees would be unwelcome "even though their work was considered to be excellent by many of the communities they served." Idaho had sixteen camps with African-American enrollees, one at Camp F-120 and nineteen African-Americans at Camp F-147. All served as kitchen helpers.[10]

In the case of African-Americans, available evidence indicates that though essentially successful, the Corps was a policy experiment of mixed outcomes. The legislation providing for the CCC specified that there should be no discrimination on the basis of "race, color, or creed,"[11] but this rule was not always honored in practice. For example, controversies over the location of camps occupied by African-Americans and their enrollment in the CCC program lasted throughout the life of the program.

This book is intended to explore such questions and in the process correct the lack of attention given to African-American participation in the CCC by examining and assessing the manner in which African-American youth were affected by the Corps in California and the actual contributions made as participants to conservation progress through their involvement in the conservation effort. Indeed, the African-American experience in California's CCC promised to illuminate sharply the interplay of recreational programs and the outlook of government bureaucrats, especially Army officers involved with CCC administration.

I first became interested in this area, in part, upon reading CCC director Robert Fechner's remark in 1935, in which he noted that racism was equally rampant, or more so, in regions outside the South. Immediately my attention turned to California as an area with the absence of the usual southern race relations and history. The African-American experience in California's CCC program confirmed Fechner's general premise that the "Negro Question" within the Corps was not confined to the states below the Mason-Dixon Line. Yet despite the problems encountered by African-Americans in California's CCC, they were able to overcome obstacles and produce some measurable results.

The subject of the Civilian Conservation Corps and the participation of African-American youth have not been closely examined by scholars of the New Deal. There are two unpublished sources that go some distance toward the recapture of the African-American experience in the CCC:

Allen F. Kifer's work still remains the most comprehensive study of African-American participation in the CCC. According to Kifer, during the first eight years of the CCC, "the New Deal had no fixed policy toward the Negro." And although the president knew of the discrimination and prejudice within the Corps, "the disturbing early years of the Civilian Conservation Corps brought no more, from the White House, than an occasional request for an investigation."[12] George Rawick maintains that while the White House was indirectly responsible for discrimination against African-Americans in the Corps, "the major responsibility for the discriminatory practices of the CCC must be shared by the CCC Administration, Robert Fechner, and the United States Army."[13] The problem with Kifer and Rawick is that they focus almost entirely on racial issues in the CCC. Kifer and Rawick certainly give adequate treatment to this aspect of the African-American experience in the Corps, but they fail to address the contributions of African-American corpsmen, despite restricted opportunities.

John A. Salmond's *The Civilian Conservation Corps, 1933–1942: A New Deal Case Study* (1967) remains the best monograph on the central organization of the Corps and how it developed and operated. Although the CCC fell short of meeting the needs of African-Americans, Salmond maintains, "It did fulfill at least some of its obligations toward unemployed American Negro youth." However, in the final analysis, he concludes, "the Negro never gained the measure of relief from the agency's activities to which his economic privation entitled him." Although Salmond highlights the problems of African-Americans in general in the Corps, he adds little to our understanding of the difficulties and opportunities encountered at the grass-roots level—that is, the state level where, for example, CCC officials and the white population yielded to traditional prejudices that prevented African-American enrollees from participating fully in the CCC program. Salmond's study, moreover, tells us little or nothing of the social profile of the young African-Americans selected or of their experience and perceptions after leaving the CCC.[14]

Charles Johnson's article, "The Army, the Negro and the Civilian Conservation Corps: 1933–1942," published in 1972, is a critical assessment of the Army's opposition to the use of African-American reserve officers in the CCC. "This was clearly discrimination based on race," Johnson complains, "however camouflaged by appeals to decentralization, local pressures, greater wisdom, or lack of applicants." Johnson further establishes that after the CCC had been in operation for nearly a year, "blacks were found in fifty-two companies with entirely black enrollees." Despite this fact, Johnson concludes, the War Department decided to use only white officers for CCC duty.[15] But Johnson's study overlooks the day-to-day operations of those companies and the rehabilitative benefits gained by African-American enrollees in the CCC. Calvin W. Gower's 1976 article on "The Struggle of Blacks for Leadership Positions in the Civilian Conservation Corps: 1933–1942" discusses some of the problems African-Americans encountered in the CCC and specifically the obstacles faced as they attempted to obtain leadership positions in the Corps. He notes, for example, that "the efforts of blacks to gain equality of opportunity by securing leadership positions in the CCC were not very successful and reflect the general failure of blacks to obtain significant improvements for themselves during the New Deal."[16]

While these scholars have noted discrimination toward African-Americans in the CCC, they have not provided any broad revision of the traditional interpretation of the African-American experience in the Corps. Even with the increasingly broad scope of scholarly investigation of various other New Deal agencies and black America, writers continue the traditional treatment of the CCC. Three studies, Leslie A. Lacy's *The Soil Soldiers: The Civilian Conservation Corps in the Great Depression* (1976), Perry H. Merrill's *Roosevelt's Forest Army: A History of the Civilian Conservation Corps* (1981), and Edwin G. Hill's work, *In the Shadow of the Mountain: The Spirit of the CCC* (1990), indicate how little impact the scholarship on race relations and the African-American role has made upon the mainstream history of this favorite relief program of President Roosevelt. Lacy, for example, fails to go beyond "recognition" of African-Americans in the Corps when he states that although there was no single problem as great as that raised by the enrollment of African-Americans and the location of camps for them, "those blacks who were accepted learned a lot in the CCC."[17] Yet the role, experience, and contributions of African-Americans in the Corps are entirely omitted in this work, leaving the impression that black enrollees were nothing more than "invisible actors" in CCC history.

The neglect of African-Americans in the history of the CCC is repeated in Perry Merrill's study of the value of the CCC to the enrollees, their families, and the states. The primary importance of Merrill's study of the Corps is that it is the first comprehensive attempt to give the participants an opportunity to discuss the value of the CCC to themselves and their families. The ways in which the participants thought the CCC had helped them and their families are many and varied. Of the three hundred letters sent by Merrill to former enrollees, he received seventy-five affirming that the Corps did produce some measurable benefits. Indeed, the letters are well chosen to personalize the CCC experience. They tell of the wide range of educational benefits received by the respondents as well as the various methods used to conserve and protect the nation's forests. "They saw the need for and learned how to take care of soil erosion . . . and the dangerous effect of certain insects and animals upon the forest and agricultural crops." But most important, according to Merrill, "their close association with each other taught them how to get along and cooperate with their neighbors and fellowmen."[18]

While his study also contains a wealth of information, particularly statistical data on work accomplishments and CCC expenditures, one area is quite disturbing, namely, his sample of former enrollees. It is inconceivable that of the seventy-five "interesting" letters received from former enrollees, not one contained negative recollections or comments. This finding does not encourage confidence in the book as a whole, and one doubts that the evidence from former enrollees included minorities.

Hill's study of the Pacific Northwest tends to follow the same script as that of Merrill. Information and accounts from CCC veterans about their experiences in the Corps and afterward are discussed throughout much of the book. Hill's only mention of African-Americans is in his introductory remarks in which he states that although most participants were white youths, when the CCC ended in 1942, "200,000 blacks had . . . also served." Again, such a remark suggests that one looks at African-American participation only as a part of the CCC in isolation from the whole.[19]

Scholarship on the CCC persists in neglecting the nonwhite clientele and experience. And if that experience is closely studied, not only the contemporary record but also the apparent value of the CCC to African-American youths as measured in their subsequent careers and by their recollections, such "all-white" histories of the CCC would require further revision.

This book will address the CCC experience as it relates to African-American participants in California. By utilizing some of the more perceptive accounts of how the Corps operated there, along with observations of former enrollees, it is possible to recapture their experience in the CCC. Indeed a study of their participation presents an opportunity to examine an important and largely unexplored area of historical investigation.[20]

To obtain information about the lives of African-American CCC veterans in California, letters and questionnaires were sent to former enrollees or family members and others who had personal recollections of the participants after 1942. Follow-up interviews were conducted. Of the twenty-six persons who responded, thirteen were former African-American corpsmen, the remainder being family members or other CCC veterans. As a result of the letters, questionnaires, and oral interviews, there is evidence that the CCC seems to have provided the participants with the tools necessary to elevate themselves to a modest middle-class economic and social level.

It is the long-range purpose, then, of this book to: evaluate the role of African-Americans in the CCC program; examine those camps having African-American enrollees with mention of any problems in locating them; examine the localities from which these enrollees came with mention of any problems encountered pertaining to recruitment and enrollment; evaluate the various work projects performed by the corpsmen with attention given to educational and recreational activities offered at the camps; and evaluate the overall benefits gained by enrollees in such areas as education and employment.

Since scholars have written little on African-Americans in New Deal history generally and the CCC in particular, a study of these corpsmen in California will further add to an understanding of Western history, African-American history, and American history in general.

CHAPTER 1

Origin of the Civilian Conservation Corps in California

Depression and African-American Youth

In 1930 approximately one million employable young people in the United States were unable to find work. In 1933, the worst unemployment year of the Depression, over a third of the nation's 14,762,000 known unemployed were under the age of twenty-five, amounting to about five million of America's youth.[1]

Eleanor Roosevelt was especially sensitive to the plight of unemployed youth. As early as 1934 she stated: "I have moments of real terror when I think we may be losing this generation. We have got to bring these young people into the active life of the community and make them feel they are necessary."[2] According to Mrs. Roosevelt in *This I Remember*, "Harry Hopkins, then head of the WPA . . . knew how deeply troubled I had been from the beginning about the plight of the country's young people, for I had talked . . . about it a number of times."[3]

In April 1935, the *New York Times*, in one of its editorials on youth unemployment, commented on the statistics that had previously been issued by the Department of Labor and the United States Commissioner of Education. The paper editorialized that it was the youth "between the ages of 16 and 24, who seem to be having the most difficult time of it just now. More than 12,000,000 young people . . . have reached the age of unemployability since October, 1929, and a very large percentage of these have not been able to take their places as producing and contributing citizens in our society."[4] Thus, the problem of American youth became abundantly clear: thousands drifted from state to state, walking the highways or riding freight trains, in search of work.

The Civilian Conservation Corps was created by an act of Congress on March 30, 1933, and was signed into law by President Roosevelt the following day. It was the first of the so-called "alphabet agencies" established during the New Deal, and it represented the federal government's recognition that American youth had its own unique set of problems to be addressed and overcome. The establishment of the CCC was initially identified as the Emergency Conservation Work (ECW) Act but was more popularly known as the CCC through its founder, President Franklin D. Roosevelt.[5]

Robert Fechner, vice president of the American Federation of Labor and an officer on the General Executive Board of the International Association of Machinists, was chosen to head the Civilian Conservation Corps. Born in Chattanooga, Tennessee, Fechner was director of the CCC until his death on New Year's Eve, 1939. He was succeeded by his executive assistant, James J. McEntee, also a former official in the machinists union. An Advisory Council consisted of Director Fechner and one representative from each of the four government departments: War, Labor, Agriculture, and Interior.[6]

The Army's role in the operations of the CCC must be considered vital. Its task of administering the camps was, by far, the most important function of all the participating departments. Within seven weeks after President Roosevelt had signed into law the Civilian Conservation Corps, the Army had mobilized 310,000 men into 1,315 camps, "a mobilization more rapid and orderly than any in the Army's history." Indeed the Army's involvement in organizing and maintaining the Corps was considered beneficial, not only for its exposure of thousands of enrollees to small-scale military training, but for its beneficial effect on military preparedness.[7]

The Department of Labor was responsible for keeping up the strength of the camps by providing a continuous flow of men, prescribed enrollment policies, and eligibility requirements. The War Department had the responsibility of examining, processing, transporting, feeding, housing, clothing, providing entertainment for, and administration of enrollees.[8] Various technical agencies, such as the National Park Service, the U.S. Forest Service, and the California Department of Forestry, operating under the Departments of Interior and Agriculture, were responsible for locating suitable camps, selecting work projects, and supervising the work performed on the various projects.[9] The CCC administration system is outlined in Appendix A (p. 79).

The CCC was established to employ young men between the ages of seventeen and twenty-three in paramilitary work camps, usually in rural areas, where they were to undertake various conservation projects. In California the Corps was directed by the Commanding General, Ninth Corps area, U.S. Army, with headquarters at the Presidio in San Francisco. The supporting organizations were the U.S. Departments of Agriculture and Interior and the National Park Service.[10]

A corpsman was to be employed in the CCC for no longer than eighteen months. His monthly salary was thirty dollars, twenty-five of which was sent home to his family. The corpsman kept the remaining five dollars for spending money. In addition to regular wages, a corpsman received food, clothing, shelter, medical care, and educational and recreational opportunities. The CCC's purpose was to take men off the bread lines of America during the time of economic depression and provide outdoor jobs for thousands.[11]

In order to understand the development and necessity for the CCC and its importance to the nation's African-American community, recognition of the national unemployment problem is essential. In 1932, for example, more than thirteen million Americans were without jobs. The government's *Special Unemployment Census* of October 1933 estimated that 14,762,000 Americans were unemployed. In some of the larger urban areas the African-American unemployment rate was acknowledged to exceed 50 percent. However, many inaccuracies limit the use of the 1933 census as providing a general picture of unemployment at different stages of the Depression. Nancy Weiss has written that "We have no precise, reliable indices of the economic status of blacks in 1930 and 1940 . . . nor can we discern much useful information from the data on unemployment in the federal census of 1930 and 1940, since census-takers used different categories and concepts in measuring employment in each of these years."[12]

Similarly, figures are not available for the total number of Americans on public relief; but figures for the total number of African-Americans on work relief are available. In late 1933, for instance, 2,177,000 African-Americans were in families receiving relief in the United States. This figure represented about 17 percent of the total African-American population in 1930. In 1935, two years after the inauguration of President Roosevelt's relief and recovery program, the number of African-Americans on relief increased to 3,737,000, or 30 percent of the African-American population.[13]

In the 1930s, many unemployment surveys were made among adults.

For American youth, however, data on unemployment is incomplete because most young people were not employed before the Depression, and therefore, statistics on youth joblessness are not as readily traceable. Yet there are estimates that clearly reveal the plight of young African-Americans in Depression America. For example, in the early 1930s there were close to 2.5 million African-American youths under the age of twenty-five, representing 10 percent of all young people in the United States. George Rawick, who analyzed fully the data for youth unemployment in the 1930s, noted that in the 1930 United States Census, in the age group fifteen to twenty-four years who were out of work, 37.8 percent were black. In that same year, Allen Kifer has stated, African-American women under the age of twenty-five made up "thirty-six percent of the feminine work force, while their share of unemployment among women of all ages was 42.4 percent."[14]

Additional figures indicate the impact of unemployment on African-Americans in the early years of the Depression. In 1940, for example, Bruce Melvin calculated that "29 percent of Negro youth in urban communities were on relief, while only 14 percent of all white youth were so situated. . . . Although it is true that all youth black or white have in common many problems," Melvin concluded, "lack of opportunity for education, inadequate guidance and vocational training, lack of work experience to complicate their job seeking, increased leisure without adequate recreational facilities—these problems are increased for the Negro youth." Clearly, African-American youth bore a large share of the burden created by the Great Depression. As John A. Salmond put it, "By any index at all, blacks were the most deprived group in the nation, the one most urgently needing government aid."[15]

In 1930 the total population of California was recorded as 5,677,251. Of this number, the state's African-American community accounted for 81,048, or 1.4 percent. In October 1933, it was estimated that in California 413,000 persons were jobless. Of this number 63.31 percent resided in three urbanized counties of the state: Los Angeles, 41.64 percent; San Francisco, 11.53 percent; and Alameda, 10.14 percent.[16] The cities having the highest number of African-American residents were Los Angeles, Oakland, and San Francisco, each with a population of 38,894, 17,503, and 3,803, respectively.[17]

Government jobs and work projects were the largest source of new employment for African-American Californians during the Depression years.

Unfortunately, little systematic information is available about the Great Depression's economic impact on California's African-American population. However, the statistical information that is available reveals, to some extent, the effects of the Depression on the state's African-American community where unemployment and public relief were concerned. In Los Angeles, African-Americans had the highest unemployment rate of any racial group.[18] In its *Annual Report* of 1931, the National Urban League estimated that of the 106 major cities in the United States, which included Los Angeles, "The proportion of Negroes unemployed was 30 to 50 percent greater than for whites."[19] The *California Eagle*, the state's largest African-American newspaper, noted that African-Americans in the city of Los Angeles had occupied close to eleven thousand janitorial or similar positions in 1920, whereas in 1934, with a population increase of twenty-two thousand, African-Americans had fewer than three thousand such jobs. Even those families not directly affected by unemployment were indirectly affected by the loss of revenue to the city's African-American community.[20]

The data issued by the federal census in 1940 shows that the number of African-Americans on relief in Los Angeles had been somewhat above that of the rest of the nation. Approximately 30 percent of the African-American population in Los Angeles was on some form of relief during the Depression years. According to an important statistical survey, by October 1933, the number of African-Americans on relief in the entire state of California was 14,426 or 17.8 percent, as opposed to 5,667,257 or 9.8 percent of the nonblack population.[21] Writing for the California State Relief Administration in 1939, Dewey Anderson stated that the average individual receiving public assistance was "a white person." He concurred, however, that "the effect of prolonged depression and its accompanying unemployment is especially noticeable on Negroes. Of an estimated ninety-seven thousand colored people in California, approximately fourteen thousand are on relief." Anderson and other state relief officials were especially concerned that while California's African-American citizens comprised 1.4 percent of the state's residents, 4.3 percent were on the State Relief Administration's case load.[22]

The law establishing the CCC contained a clause that prohibited discrimination based on race. Yet despite instructions from National Selection director W. Frank Persons that enrollees be selected without regard to race, Corps administrators in many states refused to select a proportionate share of African-Americans. At the start of the program, African-American enrollment was restricted to less than 10 percent of the national Corps total. By 1935 African-American participation had reached 10 percent, which might be considered equitable, insofar as it corresponded to the proportion of African-Americans in the total population counted in 1930. But as Nancy Weiss points out, it was "less than adequate when measured against the disproportionate relief needs of blacks."[23]

Enrolling in the Corps was a lengthy process. Initially, the Army was responsible for selecting enrollees. However, at the first organizational meeting held at the White House on April 3, 1933, it was decided that this responsibility would be subsequently transferred to the Labor Department. The Selection Division of the Labor Department decided the quota for each enrollment period, which was usually two years, for individual states. Quotas were based on each state's population. After the Army adjutant general's office received a list of quotas from the respective states, Corps area commanders were informed of the number of men to be enrolled and the camps to which they would be assigned.[24]

The selection process had barely begun when reports were received in Washington, D.C. from several southern states that local selection officials were deliberately excluding African-Americans from admission into the CCC. In Georgia, whose population was 36 percent African-American, no non-Caucasians had been recruited into the Corps during the early weeks of its operation. It was not until W. Frank Persons, who directed CCC selection in Washington, D.C., threatened to stop all enrollment in the state unless African-Americans were included in Corps activities that Georgia began to include people of color in the CCC. Similarly, in June 1933, the state of Mississippi, with an African-American population of 50 percent, selection officials admitted only 46 African-Americans, or less than 2 percent of the total enrollment of 2,776 men.[25]

Not all of the complaints in regard to discrimination in enrollment came from southern states.[26] Seemingly, African-Americans in the West encountered fewer enrollment problems. Perhaps this was due, at least in part, to the fact that in many southern states, the issue was whether to include African-Americans at all. In the West, however, the issue was simply to secure an equitable share of CCC positions. In California, protest came from various African-American communities throughout the state. In San Francisco County in early April 1939, for instance, applicants, parents, and social organizations complained that as a result of the last-minute cancellation of the African-American requisition for the month of April, "discrimination had been shown in the matter of selection."[27] Representatives of the Booker T. Washington Community Service Center, also in the San Francisco Bay Area, responded to the cancellation by insisting that "more publicity . . . be given the colored camps as there were certainly a sufficient number of colored boys unemployed."[28] In Los Angeles, where the African-American population was the largest and the most vocal, the cancellation of April's African-American requisition created a considerable furor. State selection director Dayton Jones wrote directly to national selection director W. Frank Persons that "Colored civic leaders and newspapers devoted to the activities of the colored population of Los Angeles . . . are vigorously protesting this cancellation in view of the fact that these colored boys had all been investigated, found eligible, and certified. . . . This still does not get us away from the attitude of the colored people here that discrimination has been shown."[29]

The situation was much the same elsewhere in California. In Imperial County, near San Diego, Corps officials acknowledged that protests against unequal treatment in the enrollment system by the African-American community was warranted because, according to the county's selection director, "this is an injustice against this group who have a very serious problem on their hands in attempting to gain work."[30]

State CCC officials insisted that African-Americans' fear of experiencing racial prejudice may have contributed to their low enrollment in the Corps. However, Director Jones admitted that while fear of racial discrimination may have discouraged qualified African-American applicants, it was by no means the only factor. After making the usual inquiry, Jones reported to Persons some possible reasons why many African-Americans, particularly in the northern part of the state, were reluctant to apply for CCC jobs:

> Another thing that has hurt our bay area colored applications is the series of unfortunate happenings or incidents at Company 2923, Yucca Creek, in the Fresno District. The first of these was a fire which wiped out headquarters building, mess hall, recreation hall, etc., and what [sic] forced the enrollees to live under somewhat unfavorable circumstances for some time. Then the next thing that occurred was through the rapid turnover of company commanders because of calls to military duty, it seems that Company 2923 for a while got the poorest series of commanders that were called to duty, and there were AWOLS, desertions, delayed allotment and pay checks, and a run of all things that can occur in a camp.[31]

Former African-American enrollees, in oral interviews, related accounts that suggest that local selection agents attempted to curtail the number of African-American CCC enrollees. "I honestly believe," Claude Pierce recalled, "that those in charge of the CCC in Los Angeles were not interested in recruiting Negroes. The CCC was advertised in the newspaper, which was not available in Negro communities. I first heard of the CCC from a white family I worked for." Cleveland Jacobs remembered how he first heard of the CCC in 1934. "I didn't even know there was such a program. I heard about the 3Cs from my aunt who was in the catering business. She was told by a prominent white family here in Los Angeles after they learned that I was having a hard time finding work." "I learned of the CCC from cousins and friends," Willie Stovall recalled. "I don't know where they got the information from. I can't remember reading about it anywhere." Herbert Walters, a white enrollee who lived in Long Beach, California, when the CCC began functioning in 1933, remembered how he heard of the Corps: "To my knowledge all of the guys who could not find work knew of the CCC. I heard about the CCC from the Employment Office, or what was equivalent to it."[32]

In any event, it was evident to some CCC officials in California, from the concern expressed in many state reports as well as from protests in the African-American community, that African-American youths were not being admitted in significant numbers into the Corps.

The enrollment of African-Americans into the CCC program was one of several problems that plagued the Corps. The issue of whether to have African-American officers for black companies also was a headache for CCC officials, as well as President Roosevelt. Two African-American leaders, Walter White of the National Association for the Advancement of Colored People (NAACP) and Emmett Scott, an official at Howard University, spearheaded the movement to have African-American officers in the CCC. It was not until August 1935 that President Roosevelt instructed the Army to call up a token number of African-American reserve medical officers and chaplains for active duty in the Corps. And it was not until the summer of 1936, a year after the original directive was issued, that three African-American officers were assigned to duty with a African-American camp at Gettysburg National Military Park in Pennsylvania. There were only two African-American officers called to duty to command African-American CCC camps—one at Gettysburg, commanded by Captain

Frederick Lyman Slade, and the other at Elmira, New York, commanded by Dr. Louis King (rank unknown). No African-Americans were appointed as camp commanders in California.[33]

The Enrollees

The recruits who initially filled the CCC camps of California were mostly from other Corps areas. This was due to the numerous work projects in the public areas of California that far exceeded the available manpower. Ohio, Indiana, and Kentucky, representing the Fifth Corps area, supplied the largest number of men. New York provided a smaller number, while Nebraska, the Dakotas, Minnesota, and Missouri contributed even fewer men. The Ninth Corps area, represented by California, Nevada, and Wyoming, was also a small supplier of recruits. In California, a total of 168 CCC camps were established and occupied by enrollees, together with supporting Army and technical service staffs. Only sixty-five of the camps were actually occupied by California youth. The remaining 103 camps were staffed by Second, Fifth, and Seventh Corps areas.[34]

The CCC was an organization of unemployed youths between the ages of seventeen and twenty-three. The average age was nineteen. The recruits were most often unskilled, and frequently their parents were without work. Physically, they averaged five feet, eight inches tall and weighed 150 pounds.[35]

In California, in addition to the majority of white enrollees, there were African-Americans, Japanese, Chinese, Filipinos, and Hispanics. Japanese, Chinese, and Filipinos were not considered as minorities at the time, and thus there is practically no information relating to them in California's CCC. Other than African-Americans, Hispanics were perhaps the largest minority group in California's CCC. However, they were not regarded as "special enrollees" as were African-Americans; except for an occasional Spanish surname in official reports, Hispanics were not singled out as a group in official records and unofficial sources, and nothing systematic is known of their CCC experience.

One California company, Company 1950, at Camp Coldbrook near Azusa, California, apparently enrolled several Hispanics. Surnames such as Gonzales, Ramirez, Romero, and Gomez are especially conspicuous in the company's "off-duty" activity correspondence. In April 1937 Company 1950 had ten enrollees with Spanish surnames.[36]

A 1971 study estimated that more than 85,000 Native Americans were represented in the program of the CCC over a period of nine years. They worked on two hundred reservations in twenty-three states. The Bureau of Indian Affairs in the Department of Interior was responsible for handling all welfare, education, and training as well as planning the CCC work projects. It conducted its own camp inspections. Native American enrollees built trails and towers, cut forest lanes, landscaped, operated fish hatcheries, and maintained bridges. In short, the work projects carried out by Native Americans were basically the same as those of other corpsmen.[37]

Donald Parman has written that the treatment of Native Americans in the CCC took a different course than accorded to African-American enrollees. "Leaders in the Office of Indian Affairs became excited over the possibility of Indians participating in the newly formed CCC," he elaborated. "These officials recognized that reservations badly needed forestation improvements, soil erosion control, restoration of grazing lands, and other projects envisioned for CCC, as well as employment opportunities afforded by the new program."[38]

Apparently Native Americans played a minor role in the CCC in California. None of the sources I used for California discussed Native Americans to any extent.

Camp Assignment

Initially, African-American enrollees were assigned to CCC camps without regard to race. Indeed, it is quite possible that Director Fechner's southern roots may have contributed to his eventual decision to racially segregate enrollees. However, close scrutiny of the attitude toward African-Americans in California's CCC, together with the position of Corps officials in Washington, D.C., the U.S. Army, and indeed the Roosevelt administration, indicates that segregation and discrimination were central features of the agency's policy toward African-Americans at all levels.[39]

The writer's correspondence with men who served in the CCC in California revealed that while separate black and white camps may have been thought desirable by CCC officials, African-American enrollees were quite often assigned to white companies because of the need for additional manpower. State and local governments, as well as private citizens, on occasion requested assistance from the Corps when emergencies arose.[40] Donald Hobart, a former Army Reserve officer and CCC camp commander, observed that "the enormous drought problem in many western states and the subsequent Drought Relief Act of 1934 made it necessary to increase the number of men and CCC companies in California in order to provide assistance during the emergency." Thus, for this reason alone, the integration of African-American enrollees within predominantly white companies continued in California until August 1935.[41]

In the West, camps in California, Idaho, Utah, and Montana had the highest number of African-American enrollees, all of whom were initially enrolled in California. The out-of-state CCC companies from Idaho, Utah, and Montana were all segregated prior to being transferred to California. However, to maintain company strength, which was normally from 200 to 230 enrollees, African-American corpsmen were frequently assigned to out-of-state units. Once a "foreign company" was ordered to return to its state of origin, the African-American enrollees were reassigned to integrated units in California.

Occasionally Ninth Corps area companies returned to their state of origin and inadvertently took along a number of African-American enrollees. One such case occurred in Utah in May 1935. Upon arrival, the local hostility was so great that the African-American enrollees wrote to President Roosevelt asking to be returned to California.[42] A month later a race riot erupted at Camp Osborne Springs, Idaho, when African-American enrollees complained of being subjected to derogatory name-calling. After the disturbance had subsided somewhat, the black enrollees "had to stay on guard all night to keep white fellows from coming in." They further complained that "the towns people at Ashton did not want colored fellows in the place even if they belong to the CCC."[43] After an investigation of the matter by the Department of War, the African-American enrollees were dismissed from the Corps, which later prompted Director Fechner to write that "a mistake was made in my opinion in sending any Negroes from California to Idaho."[44] Whether justified or not, the African-Americans' dismissal from the Corps by the Army was indicative of the military's adversarial relationship with African-American corpsmen, which, as Charles Johnson has written, "had deep roots in Army tradition, reinforced by experiences during World War I."[45]

When the CCC began operating in 1933, there was no attempt to reform race relations. In the southern states, black and white enrollees were assigned to separate camps. A scholar who studied carefully the central organization of the Corps noted that, "It was never the policy of CCC officials to create a nationwide system of integrated camps. Given the custom of the era, to do so would have invited trouble."[46] From its creation, therefore, the CCC practiced segregation in the South. By 1935, however, this practice would have a far-reaching impact that would contribute to the development of a nationwide policy in regard to African-Americans in the program of the CCC.

In the northern and western states, only when there were not enough African-Americans to form separate companies were they allowed in all-white camps. In California, the integration of African-American enrollees into white companies did not appear to present major difficulties. Perhaps most of the answers lie in the internal organization of camps. Corps commanders, with encouragement from the state's Emergency Relief Administration in San Francisco, assigned African-American enrollees to menial duties to accomplish some segregation between the races. In a letter to National Selection director Persons in Washington, D.C., Dayton Jones of the Emergency Relief Administration in California, suggested how segregation could be accomplished, even though CCC regulations prohibited segregation and discrimination. Indeed, it is essential to quote Jones's letter in its entirety to show the extent to which officials in California would go to accomplish and maintain a policy of segregation in the state's CCC camps. Jones wrote:

It is a known fact that colored boys make efficient kitchen and dining-room aides, and in addition the vast majority of colored youths enjoy this type of work. By being assigned to work as cooks' helpers, kitchen police and in the preparation of raw vegetables for the men such as peeling and slicing potatoes, a good proportion of the colored members in most camps could be absorbed in this manner. Segregation of the colored boys in the mess halls is prevalent in a number of camps by virtue of actual necessity to prevent racial difficulties. Under my plan this segregation would automatically be accomplished because of the fact that kitchen help must necessarily eat at a time when other than the rest of the enrollees take their meals. By assigning these colored boys to this particular type of work the segregation could be accomplished with no one realizing that segregation was being effected.[47]

Jones recognized that this practice was contrary to the language of the legislation establishing the CCC when he wrote: "I know that segregation is frowned upon but nevertheless at present it is a real problem and this is merely a thought of mine in connection with a practice which while not recognized and admitted is a reality."[48]

The attitudes reflected above represent an example of the negative features and consequences of CCC practices toward African-American enrollees. Yet these circumstances prevailed despite the legislation that expressly forbade discrimination on the basis of race.

The effects of integration on African-American corpsmen within predominantly white companies in California were also difficult to determine. The normal factors such as production and work quality of African-American enrollees were not reported separately from those of white enrollees. They were obviously a human part of the whole social structure of the camp.

African-American enrollees were frequently utilized as cooks and kitchen helpers. One African-American participant who was assigned to Camps Bouquet Canyon, near Sangus, California, and Tuna Canyon, located south of Tujunga, California, remembered the circumstances of his camp duties: "At Bouquet I was in the kitchen crew. All blacks were in this crew. At Tuna Canyon, for awhile I was in the kitchen. Later, I was in the road crews." "I was the only black truck driver in my company," William Nelson recalled. "There was some status to being a truck driver. Some of the blacks worked in the kitchen, but whites did also." Another former enrollee assigned to a camp near Sacramento, California, noted that work assignments were divided equally among black and white corpsmen. "There were only 10 blacks in our company of about 150," he remarked, "I guess it didn't matter. My commander had been in the Navy and treated all enrollees the same. He did not discriminate."[49]

What this information suggests is that African-American corpsmen in integrated camps were not *always* assigned kitchen police or similar duties, contrary to the intent of local CCC officials.

Interviews with former enrollees, both African-American and white, who were assigned to integrated CCC camps give insight into race relations. Although CCC companies were "integrated," camps, internally, were not. In some camps, for example, dressing and work rooms, as well as dining halls, were segregated. "They had to bunk, eat and work together," stated one white participant, "and they complained a lot about segregation." "Blacks stayed in one barracks," recalled an African-American enrollee, "whites in another." One African-American enrollee remembered what it was like when he and several other African-Americans arrived at an all-white camp in September 1933: "When the group I enlisted with arrived . . . we found it was a white camp composed of enlistees from Wyoming. No blacks were expected. It was necessary to arrange a space in the barracks for us [the blacks] and the whites said a wall should be erected." A white enrollee recounted that "at Spring Flats Camp in the fall of 1933, about one fourth of the camp's enrollees were black. They were all in Barracks Four. I didn't see them too often."[50]

Interviews with several African-American enrollees who were assigned to integrated companies in California reveal that, in general, they were well treated by other corpsmen. One participant noted that "the camp that I was assigned to was approximately 85 percent white and 15 percent black. We all got along fine." William Nelson, who lived in Fresno, California, when he joined the Corps in 1933, recalled the relations between African-Americans and whites in a camp located in Sequoia National Park. "We were treated well and socialized with whites. There were some whites from Kentucky who were anti-black, but were put in line by blacks, especially those from L.A." "We got along fine with whites," another corpsman remarked, "most of the blacks in my company were from the city and had gone to school with whites." One participant noted that "a couple of fights between blacks and whites did happen. I don't believe it was because of race. The commander made them put on boxing gloves to settle the argument."[51]

As a point of comparison, one white participant summarized his view of the treatment of African-Americans and perhaps represented the general view of the matter: "Some of the white enrollees were from the south or border states. Integrating them with minorities was no easy job. We never thought the blacks were mistreated by us."[52]

Written and oral sources revealed that in integrated CCC camps and companies disciplinary problems were no more prevalent among the African-American enrollees than they were among white enrollees. Nor were more serious or critical problems found to exist among the African-American than among the white enrollees. However, during the first weeks of the agency's existence, an incident involving four African-American enrollees occurred at Camp Concow, Company 992, a reforestation facility located in a remote area of northern California. In June 1933, the story broke that when lunchtime arrived at one of the work sites, two enrollees, one white and one African-American, quarreled over a lunch kit belonging to the African-American enrollee. Just as the two enrollees were about to settle the question as to who was the rightful owner, the Forest Service foreman intervened and threatened the African-American enrollee. A reporter for the *California Eagle* described how the incident marked the beginning of a few days of "travail of the soul" for the African-American enrollees: "In attempting to force his command, Ranger Smith raised his pick in the act of striking the young colored lad, which . . . brought the colored boys on the job to Hubbard's assistance, because said the boys, the ranger was a man weighing something over two hundred pounds while Hubbard weighs about an [sic] hundred and thirty. In the scramble, the ranger fell or was knocked down, none of the boys. . . being able to determine just how it happened, for as they declared, their one and only desire was to avert trouble."[53]

The incident at Camp Concow resulted in an investigation by the director's office in Washington to verify a report of "alleged discrimination against colored enrollees in California conservation camps." The investigator's report concluded that after consideration of the testimony given and observations made at Company 992, "it is the opinion . . . that there is no racial discrimination between White and colored CCC enrollees in the above camp, by either U.S. Army officers assigned to the Company or by the U.S. Forest Service official in charge of work projects." It is also noted, parenthetically, that "the consensus of opinion is that Colored enrollees are not as amenable to discipline necessary for the proper operation of the camp."[54]

In July 1933, 125 African-American and white enrollees deserted the Bear River reforestation camp located in the Sierra Nevada near Sacramento, California.[55] The Army's investigation of the matter led to the suspicion that the camp's African-American enrollees were responsible for the incident, despite the lack of evidence. In a letter to President Roosevelt's secretary, Colonel Louis Howe, the investigating officer, E. M. Duncan, remarked that "I still feel as we say in the Southland, there is a nigger in the wood pile."[56] Needless to say, the investigator's report revealed a racist attitude in certain areas of CCC activity—notably elements within the U.S. Army Officer's Corps.[57]

At Camp Palomar Mountain in the Cleveland National Forest, there was a racially inspired incident in July 1935. It was alleged that a group of "white-sheeted" enrollees attacked enrollees who associated with African-Americans. The mess steward was thrown in a garbage receptacle, and the assistant company clerk was brutally beaten. The disturbance caused a total breakdown of what morale there was at the camp.[58]

Also during the early days of the CCC there was allegedly a racially motivated riot in a camp near Chico, California, which led to the dismissal of twelve African-American enrollees. Unfortunately, I was unable to verify the authenticity of the incident. However, according to one African-American enrollee who was assigned to one of many CCC camps located in the Lassen National Forest near Chico, the purported riot resulted from bigoted elements within the city of Chico and the failure of the Forest Service to provide adequate recreational facilities. "The blacks who went there did not know how to mix with white people," he explained. "It was a bigoted community. Nothing for the blacks to do, no sports, no women, nothing."[59] In any event, if true, the aforementioned incidents were the only instances of trouble involving black enrollees during the period of integration.

The Corps did all it could do to cover up enrollee disturbances, for it knew the negative publicity would certainly tarnish its image, its appeal to establish American principles, its positiveness, and indeed, its popularity with the "home folks." Few, if any of the incidents involving African-American enrollees got press coverage or caused disruption to normal camp operations.

The impact of the CCC on California communities could not be determined during those early days when enrollees were assigned to camps without regard to race. Many camps were located in extremely remote areas of the state, in which recreation was limited to a choice of in-camp activities or long frequently unrewarding trips to small, white, and often racist communities. In such cases, the African-American enrollees chose to remain in camp and engage in the limited in-camp recreational activities. In some cases, particularly where the community was supported by logging or lumber industries, small, isolated (segregated) African-American communities were to be found. In these instances, African-American enrollees were always welcomed and able to find sources of recreation and entertainment.

A few of the recruits did express views on community reactions to African-American corpsmen. One enrollee who was assigned to Camp Mill Creek, near Red Bluff, California, observed that "when I was in a mixed company I was treated OK wherever I went. I didn't go to places where I knew I wasn't welcome. I knew I was black and acted as such." "When we went to Santa Barbara," another stated, "we were treated fine. I guess it was because they knew we were not going to stay." Walter Jacobs recalled his frequent visits to Riverside, California, while assigned to Camp Palomar Mountain. "I went to Riverside often because I had a girlfriend there. Blacks from our camp went to dances and played baseball in Riverside, and there was never any trouble." According to one participant, there was an instance when a nearby community made it known that African-American enrollees were unwelcome, even in the company of whites. He recounted visiting Taft, California, a small rural community south of Fresno: "A few of us blacks and a number of whites were returning to camp and decided to stop in Taft. As we entered the city a sign read, 'Read nigger and run; if you can't read—run anyway. Nigger don't let the sun go down on you in Taft.'" The importance of this experience is that it remained vivid in the memory of the former enrollee. Many years later he is still able to remember the entire wording on the sign. "Even today when I visit Fresno," he remarked, "I make it a point to by-pass Taft."[60]

Early on, African-American enrollees had been distributed to predominantly white units throughout the Ninth Corps area. In the late summer of 1934, however, the commander of the Ninth Corps area, Major General Malin Craig, complained to Fechner about the large number of African-Americans being shipped to the Ninth Corps area, especially from the state of New York. The commander was unhappy "with the situation into which he had been pushed."[61] The presence of so many "city boys" in the West was creating a problem.

Pressure from local communities to isolate blacks from white enrollees forced Fechner to push increasingly for segregation as a matter of policy. Evidence of local opposition to racially mixed CCC camps in the West is apparent in the following letter, dated April 26, 1935, from a concerned mother in the community of Brigham City, Utah, to Governor Henry H. Blood: "At present the War Department has stationed a very undesirable class of men, such as Mexicans, Phillipians [sic] and, worst of all, Negroes. Imagine the social problems this incurs in our city. As a mother of two growing daughters, whose property and home joins this camp, I implore your support and influence in having this group of men moved from our community."[62]

Yet it was not until Fechner traveled West that his decision to separate the races would become practice. The decision to "deintegrate" was clearly illustrated in this excerpt of a letter from Fechner to California's CCC Selection director Dayton Jones:

> From the very start of the Emergency Conservation work I decided the negro and white enrollees should be segregated and this policy was generally followed in all Corps Areas. About a year ago I made an extensive trip through a number of western states visiting CCC camps and I learned of some of the unfortunate relationships that existed in some of the camps where there was a mixture of white and negro enrollees. I have also learned of the vigorous resentment shown by some communities where a considerable number of negro enrollees were placed.[63]

What the letter indicates is that the director had made the decision to segregate even before the "Negro Question" in the CCC became an issue. Thus, with antipathy from local communities, the racist attitude of the Army and Fechner's southern origins, along with the usual racial fears, the decision was made to separate black and white enrollees, a decision, as one scholar has written, "in which President Roosevelt concurred."[64]

The policy announced in July 1935 ordered: "Complete segregation of white and colored enrollees is directed. Only in those states where the colored strength is too low to form a company unit will mixing of colored men in white units be permitted."[65]

Almost immediately the director's office was deluged with complaints from groups and individuals in California asking for a change in policy. Some, in fact, complained directly to President Roosevelt. In September 1935 the Los Angeles Inter-Denominational Ministers' Alliance petitioned Roosevelt "and the organization directly in charge Not to Establish and separate or segregate branches of the CCC in California" because "separate or segregated branches of the CCC will tend to militate against the best interests of the Negroes in California." Two months later the same group appealed to James J. McEntee, Fechner's executive assistant, stating "we sincerely hope that the policy will be changed and that no segregated

Camps will be established." McEntee replied: "From experience it appears that segregation is desirable for the happiness, contentment and general welfare of the colored enrollees."[66]

California congressman Thomas Ford also participated in the controversy surrounding the racial makeup of CCC camps and the possible political repercussions. In a letter to Fechner, Ford complained: "I am receiving many and loud complaints in regard to the recent order segregating colored enrollees in the CCC camps in California. May I have an explanation of this with the expressed approval of any colored leaders, if you have such approval. As a member of Congress who has 40,000 colored voters, I am naturally concerned. Personally I have always been opposed to race segregation."[67]

Even so, the central office in Washington maintained that after a careful investigation of the matter and consultation with representative individuals and groups interested in the work of the CCC, "the decision to segregate . . . was generally approved."[68]

Agitation over the policy of segregation in the CCC prompted the NAACP to complain to Director Fechner. Thomas L. Griffith, Jr., president of the Los Angeles branch of the NAACP, vigorously protested to Fechner and the White House that "we do not feel that circumstances justify the separation of the races." He further noted that the local office as well as the national office in New York were "anxiously awaiting a reply from President Roosevelt, whether it is the policy of the Federal Government to establish the separate camps . . . and the cause for the establishment of these camps." Fechner insisted, however, that "nothing has come to this office from California . . . showing any general dissatisfaction . . . with the policy." He concluded: "I am confident the negro enrollees themselves are thoroughly satisfied with the arrangement."[69]

However, oral interviews with participants revealed that not many, if any, were particularly happy with the decision to segregate. In fact, some of the former enrollees who were discharged prior to the order were unaware of the decision and were thoroughly surprised that it had been made. One former recruit remembered what it meant to blacks at Camp Palomar Mountain: "There was only twelve of us at Palomar Mountain. We were never told why we were being transferred out. It was not until we got to Camp Piedra Blanca that we realized what was going on. I didn't like it, but I didn't understand it more than anything else." "My concern was would we get the same amount of money as the whites," noted another enrollee assigned to a mixed company at Camp Mill Creek. "It didn't bother me until later," he continued, "but like I said, at the time I knew the rules and didn't break them." One participant who was discharged in early 1935 remarked: "I didn't learn about it until years later. We got along fine with whites at Lassen [National Forest], so I figured everything else was OK elsewhere." "I'm surprised to hear of it," noted another. "Why did they do it?" A former Reserve Officer in the CCC at the time recalled the reaction of whites to the decision to separate recruits: "When black enrollees were told that they had to leave, many whites objected and wanted an explanation. Neither the black nor white enrollees were ever given an explanation as to why the blacks were being transferred out of the camps."[70]

Available evidence indicates that President Roosevelt never responded to Griffith's concerns, nor to those of the national office. And despite protests from the NAACP, California camps remained segregated, for what the director's office regarded as the good of the CCC and blacks.

In the summer of 1935, Ninth Corps area headquarters in San Francisco instructed all CCC districts in California with African-American enrollees assigned to integrated companies to transfer them for the "formation of five colored companies in California," effective August 9, 1935. The directive also stipulated that companies with African-American corpsmen transfer the proportional share of existing company funds to the new companies.[71] Throughout the remaining seven years of the Corps, racially segregated camps were the norm. In 1942, when the CCC was officially terminated, almost all of the African-American corpsmen in California had at one time been assigned to one of the all-African-American companies.

CHAPTER 2

African-American CCC Companies
in California, 1935–1942

Four African-American CCC companies were established in southern California during the fall of 1935, two of which were in Los Angeles County. The two Los Angeles County companies spent the fall months constructing and maintaining forest service roads. Between 1935 and 1942 there were five African-American companies located throughout the state of California: Company 2922-C, F-157; Company 2923-C, F-164; Company 2924-C, F-140; Company 2925-C, P-295; and Company 2940-C, SP-4. Letters of designation identified both the type of camp and the agency administering it. CCC projects in California were divided into four major categories: State Park Camps (SP), National Forest Camps (F), State Forest Camps (P), and National Park Camps (NP). War Department Army officers managed the day-to-day operations of the camps, which were coordinated by a state CCC director. A civilian projects superintendent assumed responsibility for the various work projects, which were administered through the U.S. Forest Service.[1]

The African-American Companies at Work

Company 2940-C

The first of the African-American companies organized was Company 2940-C, at Camp San Pablo Dam, located in the East Bay Municipal Utility District Recreation Area in Richmond, California, about ten miles north of Oakland. Company 2940-C, under the command of Captain Russell Louden, occupied Camp San Pablo Dam on August 1, 1935. The work projects undertaken by the company included construction and maintenance of park roads, development and maintenance of picnic ground facilities, reduction of fire hazards, beautification of the park, long-range protection of the watershed, and the control of forest fires. The average number of men assigned to this and other camps at any one time was 150.[2]

The organization of Company 2940-C posed problems quite removed from the norm. The African-American companies in southern California were organized by the transfer of white enrollees out of racially mixed camps; African-American enrollees were transferred in to occupy the vacant spaces until there was a total of four African-American companies. One of the African-American companies was filled as a result of the transfer of enrollees from CCC camps in the Fresno district, as well as an increase in enrollment.[3]

Such was not the case for 2940-C, however. As a newly organized company, it had no enrollees to transfer out, and the problem of bringing enrollees in was different from that of southern California units, which drew large numbers from other CCC camps. Company 2940-C acquired approximately 233 enrollees from 39 different companies, all of which were located in the Sierra National Forest.

The immediate task in establishing the camp at San Pablo Dam was to form an effective and efficient camp administration and technical workforce of enrollees, most of whom had not previously been given the opportunity to demonstrate the skills and activities necessary to operate a CCC camp. For the first time, African-American enrollees in California were being assigned to positions of authority and responsibility, such as squad leader, company clerk, assistant educational adviser, heavy equipment operator, as well as being assigned to work crews where such skills as carpentry, electrical repair, painting, and various phases of road and trail construction and soil conservation practices and techniques were used.[4]

While Company 2940-C was assigned to Camp San Pablo Dam, the enrollees were prohibited from entering the nearby city of Richmond. Protests had been made to the Richmond Police Department concerning the African-American camp off San Pablo Dam Road, and letters requesting the removal of the African-American enrollees had been sent to Senator W. G. McAdoo (D-Calif.) After months of community harassment, including several "official visitations" from so-called responsible citizens committees from the Richmond community, the district commander made the decision to disband Company 2940-C, transfer all enrollees to one or more of the southern California companies, and immediately reestablish Company 2940-C as a white company.[5]

An enrollee assigned to Camp San Pablo Dam recalled, "We all knew that we were not welcome in Richmond. We were always welcome in Oakland and that's where we went most of the time for recreation." An enrollee from San Diego remarked that "we knew the reputation Richmond had so we all went to Oakland or San Francisco where we were very welcome."[6]

Company 2923-C

Elsinore, California, was the site of Camp La Cienega, where corpsmen worked in the Cleveland National Forest. The men of 2923-C carried out numerous and diversified assignments.[7] Major work projects included pine beetle control and containing a wild elk herd within the Laguna Plateau Reserve. The company, under the command of Captain Kenneth P. Jones, also fought many forest fires, including several major ones: the 1935 Malibu Mountain and Brown Mountain fires, both in the Los Angeles National Park; the 1936 Cajon Canyon and Lake Arrowhead and Crestline fires, both in the San Bernardino National Forest; and the North Creek and Ramona fires, both in the Cleveland National Forest. Company 2923-C, known as "The Busy-Bee Company," had a reputation for not only taking on difficult projects but also for traveling throughout southern California to battle forest fires.[8]

Company 2923-C remained at Camp La Cienega for approximately three years. During its stay, there were several personnel changes—the Corps having been organized as a training ground for the reserve officers. Also, due to maximum length of service limitations set for all enrollees other than exempted specialists, project assistants, and local experienced men (LEMs), approximately six hundred enrollees passed through 2923-C while stationed at Camp La Cienega.

On October 9, 1938, 2923-C vacated La Cienega, and the facility was abandoned as a permanent CCC camp. The company moved to occupy Camp San Pablo Dam, an unusually picturesque site located in the East Bay hills above the city of Richmond, California. The company continued to carry out beautification projects in what is today Samuel P. Taylor State Park, in addition to the routine fire hazard reduction and road and campground construction and maintenance.[9]

In the summer of 1939, Company 2923-C vacated Camp Pablo Dam. As a result of community harassment and intimidation, the district commander of Sacramento CCC district made the decision to remove the company from San Pablo Dam and to occupy Camp Yucca Creek, a permanent

Fig. 1. Company 2923-C, Camp La Cienega, F-164. Elsinore, Calif.

Members

Reading from left to right—

FIRST ROW: J. Macon, K. Field, R. White, R. Lee, H. Barton.

SECOND ROW: C. Warfield, E. Kennedy, C. Fields, E. Peters, M. Morris, B. Williams, L. Ramirez, C. Adams, L. Davis, W. Ross, J. Avery, H. Stroud, W. Jones.

THIRD ROW: C. Bethel, S. Cobb, E. Johnson, W. Kirk, T. Foster, S. Henderson, E. Swanson, F. Wilson, W. McDaniel, J. Smyles, G. Coats, C. Johnson, E. A. Raby, Jr.

FOURTH ROW: J. A. Tabb, Jr., R. Battle, S. Lockett, B. T. Williams, J. High, H. Murray, L. Milan, H. Magee, L. Johnson, J. Coleman, I. Jones, M. Harris, J. Roberts, W. Parker.

FIFTH ROW: F. Burt, E. Kelly, P. Popoff, L. Goff, T. Pina, M. Ramsey, C. Ballesteros, A. Seeger, L. Aparicio, J. Binkerd, D. Flores, J. Lares, R. Hale.

Officers

CAPT. KENNETH P. JONES, Inf-Res. . . . *Commanding Officer*
FIRST LT. JOHN W. BEHYMER, CA-Res. . . . . . . *Adjutant*
FIRST LT. ALTON G. HUGHES, Med-Res. . . . *Camp Surgeon*
THOMAS L. JACKSON . . . . *CEd*

Technical Personnel

RAY C. SMITH . . . . *Project Superintendent*
R. FERGUSON   C. McDONALD
C. HAYES   E. KERFOOT
                C. DUCKERING

Fig. 2. Company 2923-C, Camp La Cienega, F-164 (continued).

Members

Reading from left to right—

FIRST ROW: W. Jones, R. Lewis, E. Thompson, D. Meyers, C. Harris.

SECOND ROW: W. Richardson, E. L. Granberry, T. Gory, J. Webb, D. Dunn, L. Fears, R. Driscoll, G. Fite, E. Johnson, B. Morris, W. Normand, J. Lowe.

THIRD ROW: W. Thomas, L. Shade, J. Lambert, D. Reedon, W. J. H. Green, W. Haywood, J. Fuller, G. Grant, W. Gibson, M. Madison, W. Ayres.

FOURTH ROW: J. Finley, R. De Grate, C. Ladd, H. Wilkinson, J. Simpkinson, E. Richardson, D. Akers, B. Wong, Q. Fork, R. Coleman, M. Stuart, M. Williams, J. Perris.

FIFTH ROW: J. McCleary, R. Jones, W. Paulsen, W. Woodcock, N. Ludolph, J. Clark, R. Mitchell, L. Choate, D. Kitchen, C. McBurnie, D. Maxfield, G. Trimble, R. Griggs.

Members Not in Picture

A. Allen, R. Allen, J. Barnes, R. Beary, H. Binns, J. Bishop, S. Boswell, F. Bowdre, D. Brown, J. Brown, R. Bruce, O. Butler, F. Chaney, K. Clark, F. Cook, J. Cooper, L. Cooper, W. Cotterell, L. Davis, O. Davis, R. D'hue, W. Easley, N. Edwards, H. Elam, J. Green, L. Handy, C. Hanley, B. Hardy, G. Harris, H. Higdon, J. Horton, C. Howard, M. Howell, A. Jones, S. Kemper, C. Lockhart, J. Martin, G. Mason, P. McClendon, D. McKinney, J. Millbrooks, R. Miller, S. Miller, F. Moore, S. Morgan, D. Morris, R. Morrison, C. Nash, J. Newman, M. Nickerson, E. Parks, L. Wright, E. Radcliffe, G. Renkins, F. Roberts, E. Robinson, R. Robinson, L. Russel, S. Salisbury, J. Scott, L. Sims, C. Smith, J. Smith, L. Smith, W. Smith, L. Spight, J. Stearns, E. Stokes, W. Taylor, H. Thomas, J. Thornton, V. Tidwell, W. Trigg, J. Turner, J. Walker, F. Waller, C. White, L. White, W. White, C. Williams, E. Williams, A. Willis, C. Woodard, E. Young.

Fig. 3. Company 2923-C, Camp La Cienega. Overview.

1. A view of the camp square.
2. The Camp Overhead.
3. The brass band.
4. E. C. W. trucks.
5. Camp La Cienega champion basketball team.
6. Carrier pigeons.
7. The radio station.
8. The cooks and K. P.'s.
9. Receiving typing instructions.
10. Leaders and assistant leaders.
11. The buglers.

service camp located in nearby Sequoia National Park. The company assimilated well and became a part of the park service and maintenance program. Work projects completed by Company 2923-C included park road and trail construction, park campground and picnic development and maintenance and general park upkeep. During the winter months, projects included all regular work, as weather conditions allowed, and also snow removal from roads that had to be kept open.[10]

For twenty-seven months, Company 2923-C remained at the Yucca Creek facility until the decision was made to reduce the Sequoia National Park allotment of CCC camps to one. When the company was transferred to another location within the park, Camp Yucca Creek was abandoned. From there the company moved to Camp Marble Fork, one of the oldest CCC camps in Sequoia National Park. The company occupied this camp on a temporary basis and continued to perform the same duties.[11]

In the winter of 1941, Company 2923-C was transferred to Camp Pinnacles, a barracks-type camp located in Pinnacles National Monument. The company's work projects included general upkeep and maintenance. The company remained at Camp Pinnacles until it was transferred to Company 2924-C, Camp Pine Valley, which was located in the Cleveland National Forest.[12]

Company 2924-C

Company 2924-C was organized at Camp Castaic when Company 2924 was disbanded as regular (white) California company. Camp Castaic was one of the first CCC camps established in the Angeles National Forest.[13] It was located in the forested area of Soledad Canyon, about fifteen miles northeast of the town of Saugus, California. Like the other African-American companies, 2924-C spent most of its time constructing and maintaining campgrounds. The company, under Captain Allen Chapman, served at Camp Castaic until the summer of 1936, when it was moved to Camp Minnewawa, a tent facility located near the Mexican border.

Although Camp Minnewawa was organized as one of the early CCC camps in California, it did not have the facilities that were typical of a barracks-type camp. In fact, Camp Minnewawa was considered one of the least desirable CCC camps in the state. The only permanent buildings in the facility were the mess hall, a building with offices and a supply room, an infirmary, a shower house, and a latrine. However, the district com-

Fig. 4. Company 2924-C, Camp Minnewawa, P-233. Jamul, Calif.

Members

Reading from left to right—
FIRST ROW: Jacob C. Peyton, John L. Brantford, Howard D. Drisdon, Sydney J. Dearborn, Robert C. Daniels, Robert W. Robinson, Gideon P. Vessell, King Robinson, Kermit J. Jefferson, Edgar A. Wylie, Jerry Mikell, Robert W. Reed, Marion H. Webb, Willie Barnett, John L. Stallworth, Lonnie Pitts.

SECOND ROW: Vernon H. Wysinger, Joe Bagsby, Robert L. Johnson, Conrad Anson, Francis E. Hill, Tommie Matthews, Semon Hardaway, Eddie Champine, Lester M. Williams, Clifford T. Myers, Frank Jamison, John E. Stokes, Albert Harrington, Harold Marshall, George Williams, Marcus G. Taylor.

THIRD ROW: James J. Hill, Warren C. Shelby, Paul T. Jones, Chester A. Maryland, Joe Logan, Howard Hill, Harold S. Hankerson, Clarence B. Hill, William B. Harris, Horace P. Slaughter, John D. Minor, Jesse Cabrera, Raymond L. Hornsberry, Coy Clardy, Robert Morrow, Marvin L. Abbott.

FOURTH ROW: Jack Smith, Henry S. Grigsby, James H. Chambers, Lloyd D. Williams, Alge M. Graves, Albert L. Critton, Fred Parks, Curtis Branom, James E. Wells, George H. Wortham, Horace W. Highshaw, Douglas L. Stephens, Clarence Ferguson, Charles W. Osborne, Ralph C. Manuel, Harold P. Flowers, Charles W. Parks.

Officers

CAPT. W. R. SEMPLE, CA-Res.	*Commanding Officer*
FIRST LT. JOSEF O. STOFT, Med-Res.	*Junior Officer*
SECOND LT. HYMAN BRUSS, 323rd Cav.	
	Transportation, Supply and Store Officer
ROY PERRY	*CEA*
OFFUTT T. MCWILLIAMS	*Director*

Technical Personnel

ROBERT C. DUGAN	*Project Superintendent*
JAMES GLENN	RAY LAMB
HERBERT BLOOMQUIST	JACK KESSLER
RICHARD GRONINGER	CLIFFORD C. CLARK
ED LOUSALET	ANDREW CLAGGETT
MARVIN TEHAN	FRED NOBLE
BERT ROLSTON	

mander, Major Louis H. Thompson, Los Angeles CCC District, assured Captain Chapman that steps would be taken to make Camp Minnewawa a comfortable permanent home for Company 2924-C.[14]

In the fall of 1936, Captain Irving Taber replaced Captain Chapman as commanding officer of the company. The appointment was supposed to represent a "new day" for Camp Minnewawa, primarily because the district commander had authorized the new commander to replace the old buildings and tents that had been in use since 1933. However, written sources indicate that Captain Chapman's dismissal as company commander may have been racially motivated. One African-American instructor at Camp Minnewawa complained directly to President Roosevelt that Captain Taber had informed him that Captain Chapman was dismissed as commander "because Chapman thought too much of Negroes. . . . No arrangements were made for us by him. He has ordered that we are to be segregated in the mess hall also. This action has caused quite a disturbance both in camp and the city of San Diego. Just two weeks ago, there was a banquet given in Glendale, California, for company commanders and educational advisors of the CCC camps in California. They were to pay three dollars a date. Our advisor, Mr. W. W. Robinson, sent his fee in. After two weeks, Major E. A. Easley, Dis. Commander of the Los Angeles Dis., sent him, Mr. Robinson, a letter telling him not to attend in that colored were not wanted."[15] This is an insightful letter in that it reveals the reality of the Army's attitude toward African-Americans: the vast majority of the Army Officer Corps had no intention of using the CCC to alter America's racial policies.

Fig. 5. Company 2924-C, Camp Minnewawa, P-233 (continued).

Members

Reading from left to right—

FIRST ROW: James B. Henry, Elmer Edwards, Samuel Crawford, Oscar McClain, George R. Graca, Marvin R. Cockrell, Virgil Franklin, Alvin Penny, Claude Thompson, Alworth T. Stokes, Robert T. Holton, Elmer G. Starr.

SECOND ROW: John W. Woods, George W. Seagraves, Harold G. Bertram, Winston O. Weston, William White, Joseph A. Clark, Franklin E. Wilson, Clyde Pounds, Robert L. Person, Thomas L. Bennett, Irving J. Holley, George E. Lovett, Manuel Manteca, Dewitt Lawrence, Horace E. Smith, Jr.

THIRD ROW: Clyde Johnson, Richard A. Doolan, Oscar Davis, Clifford T. Morton, George Jackson, Stewart C. Martin, David B. Coulter, Albert E. Simpson, Moses Kelley, Sidney J. Hayles, Lexie V. Ashley, Henry Williams, Julius Keys, Alfred Brown, Leorn Cooper, Claude L. Matthews, Woodrow B. Hyde.

FOURTH ROW: Mario Araujo, Alexander Majors, Wilson T. Dennis, John Synagogue, Lawrence E. Edwards, Lloyd Eason, Mack Robinson, Willie H. Jackson, Cornelius Frazier, Edward McLain, Freddie Smith, Alfred Deal, William E. Hall, Michael M. McDow, Raymond Johnson, Tennie M. May, Jr., Joe N. Roberts.

FIFTH ROW: Aaron E. Bell, John Murray, Charles Williams, Howard Revere, Clyde Burnett, Herbert J. King, Lawyer Bell, Frederick H. Weaver, Merle F. Bass, Howard Lewis, Thomas H. Ealey, Alfred Dill, Jessie Suanks, Jr., Robert W. Starks, Arthur J. Giles.

Members Not in Picture

Daniel Broiles, Samuel Washington, Raymond E. Sorsby, Alvin A. Allen, Leon Wilson.

Fig. 6. Company 2924-C, Camp Minnewawa. Overview.

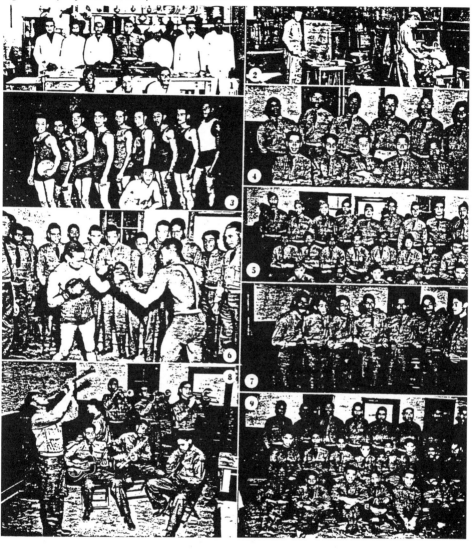

1. Cooks in the kitchen.

2. Enrollees in a workshop.

3. The basketball team.

4. The telephone crew.

5. The camp leaders.

6. Enrollees enjoying a boxing match.

7. The chorus.

8. The orchestra.

9. The Camp Overhead.

From Camp Minnewawa, the company moved to Camp Pine Valley, located in the Cleveland National Forest, about forty-five miles east of San Diego. Camp Pine Valley, designed as the permanent service camp for the Cleveland National Forest, was old and dilapidated. In use since 1933, it was the first CCC camp to be occupied in California. The work projects

Fig. 7. Company 2924-C, Camp La Cienega. Tecate and Horno side camps.

1. Horno Side Camp group.
2. Tecate Side Camp group.
3. The truck drivers.
4. Fred Noble and Bert Rolston—The Technical Personnel.
5. A view of the main camp.
6. The infirmary at the main camp.

undertaken by Company 2924-C consisted of maintaining and repairing Forest Service roads and truck trails and the construction of fire breaks. When the CCC officially ended in 1942, the company remained assigned to the facility at Pine Valley until July 1942.

Company 2925-C

Camp Topanga Canyon, a tent facility, was established in Topanga, California, nine miles south of the community of Canoga Park. This camp had been previously occupied by two out-of-state companies. Although Company 2925-C occupied this site for only a short period, it had to assign a crew to the task of making the camp livable. This crew was also on call for fire suppression.[16]

Fig. 8. Company 2925-C, Camp Piedra Blanca, F364. Wheeler Springs, Calif.

Members

Reading from left to right—

FIRST ROW: Willie Daniels, Jr., Roy McNeair, Robert E. House, William F. Arbuckle, Lucius Fleet, Forrest Tobin, Clyde Williams, Geenie Williams, Robert L. Mathis.

SECOND ROW: Thessie Jones, Robert J. Gunn, William E. Nicholson, Jr., Louis Johnson, Frederic L. Harris, Lennis Guidry, Walter Perkins, James Campbell, Edward Freeman Stewart, Phillip Oglesby, Alfred Williams, Eugene Johnson.

THIRD ROW: Maxwell Milton Hutchins, Walter O. Watson, Jr., James Allison, George Williams, Joseph Anderson, James Baldwin, Pauk Postell, Manuel D. Tally, Claude F. Pierce, Charles Williams, Timothy Mitchell, James Waller, Bill Roger, Joseph Ferjia.

FOURTH ROW: Marion Campbell, Otis Williams, John Prade, Leroy Carpenter, Alexander W. Flood, Robert Hutson, Sherman H. Jones, Harry Douglas, Philander Smith, Vernon K. Mullen, Frederick Jenkins, Joseph Reed, Charles Mason, Ageroldo Catherill, Edwin Kennedy.

Officers

CAPT. C. K. NIBLACK, CA-Res. . . . . *Commanding Officer*
SECOND LT. JESTIN L. SPACKMAN, CA-Res. . . . *Junior Officer*
E. W. SCOTT . . . . *Contract Surgeon*
DR. ROY PERRY . . . . *CEA*
MR. TEAGARDEN . . . . *EEP Teacher*

Technical Personnel

MR. C. M. BROWN . . . . *Project Superintendent*
   MR. GERALD KEMPER   MR. JACK CHILDRETH
   MR. ARTHUR ELLIS   MR. SAM KOSUB

Fig. 9. Company 2925-C, Camp Piedra Blanca, F364 (continued).

Members

Reading from left to right—

FIRST ROW: Eugene Williams, Larence Williams, Marshall R. Simmons, Jr., Terry Johnson, Jewel S. Yarber, Joseph C. McCoy, William A. Sweet, William A. Bush, Kenneth W. Sanford, Euradell Hendricks, Hosea Bolan, Welsey Smith.

SECOND ROW: Alvin Barnes, Edward Harris, Raymond Hogen, Lawrence Ebow, Melvin Samuels, Lionel G. McQuillon, John Henry Logan, Albert H. Sprow, Elwood Cobb, William Weston.

In the fall of 1935, Company 2925-C was transferred from Camp Topanga Canyon to Camp Alta Loma. This was a permanent, barracks-type camp located some five miles north of the community of Alta Loma, California. The regular activities of the company were limited because the work crews were frequently called out to fight forest fires, and as a result, Company 2925-C accomplished little road maintenance.[17]

After leaving Camp Alta Loma, the company, under Captain William E. Story, moved to Camp Kenworthy, one of the first CCC camps established in the San Bernardino National Forest. Although the principal assigned work projects were construction and maintenance, the most time-consuming task was fire fighting. In the first few months on site, Company 2925-C spent more time fighting forest fires than on regular work projects. Major fires included the Lake Arrowhead and Crestline, Hewitt Ranch, Sawpit Canyon, Seeley Ranch, and San Servaune Canyon.[18]

Fig. 10. Company 2925-C, Camp Piedra Blanca. Overview.

1. The camp boxers.

2, 4, 5, 6, 7. Groups of enrollees including the Camp Overhead, classes in Commerce, and Bible, truck drivers, and the Rennaissance Club.

3. The basketball team.

8. The cooks and K. P.'s.

9. The camp quartet.
   Left to Right: Morton, Dawes, Harris, Kennedy.

10. Boxer Strong with his trainer and manager.

11. The camp pet.

In October 1937, Company 2925-C departed Camp Kenworthy and moved to Camp Piedra Blanca, located in the Santa Barbara National Forest (later renamed Las Padres National Forest). Some of the enrollees identified themselves as the Black Boys from "White Rock." While assigned to Camp Piedra Blanca, Company 2925-C carried out erosion-control projects, which included removing fire hazards, cleaning up flammable debris, and constructing drainage ditches and channels. The company served at Camp Piedra Blanca until it was transferred to Camp Mt. Pinos, also in the Las Padres National Forest.[19]

Unlike other camps previously discussed, Camp Piedra Blanca was inundated with numerous internal problems. Accusations of inefficiency with racial overtones, charges of discrimination, complaints regarding poor recreational facilities, and charges of favoritism plagued the camp. One enrollee sent an anonymous letter to Director Fechner alleging that the camp commander was a racist. He complained and asked for an investigation:

> We are asking you to investigate the gross injustice and deprivation of our civil and constitutional rights by our commanding officer, Captain Elbert W. A. Taylor. We are redicued [sic] by the captain and are told that we need a taste of the rope around our neck and the tar and feather treatment as given the Negro in the South. . . . He speaks to us Colored boys as if we were no more than dogs and tells us we should be back in slavery. He will call one of us a black sun [sic] of a bitch in a minute. This we resent and feel that it will lead to something drastic in the very near future if immediate actions are not taken.[20]

This very serious charge prompted an investigation. The investigating officer concluded that the company commander was in fact "prejudiced against enrollees and indifferent to their welfare," and that there was a "lack of sufficient recreational and athletic facilities." The commander, Captain Elbert Taylor, was transferred to another camp and replaced by Captain Charles Black.[21]

Company 2922-C

The remaining African-American company, 2922-C, worked primarily on public campground development and maintenance. Company 2922-C was organized in August 1935 at Camp City Creek, near Highland, California. The company spent only four months at City Creek, after which all 232 enrollees were transferred to other African-American companies in California. Although the reason for the massive transfer remains vague, and the available sources provide no firm verification, community resistance could have been the motivating factor in disbanding the company. Shortly after the disbandment of 2922-C in January 1936, a California white company was transferred in. Camp City Creek remained on the roster until as late as August 1941, always occupied by a white company.[22]

Special Projects in California

Although most CCC companies in California, which averaged about 150 men each, performed a variety of tasks, some were assigned to special work projects, that is, priority tasks that made major contributions to California and the overall status of CCC programs. For example, in March 1937, Camp Dalton Canyon, a white camp, was selected to manufacture concrete cribbing to be used on truck trails in the Angeles National Forest. A special CCC cribbing plant turned out between three and four thousand pieces of concrete, which were used on the Monroe, Big Dalton, and Saw-Pit-Monrovia Truck Trails. Some of the cribbing was sent to other camps to be used in the construction of trails. Company 1950, Camp Coldbrook, also a white company located in the Angeles National Forest, worked on the largest campground project in the state. During the fire season of 1936 the company's suppression crew, the so-called "Fighting Fifties," was dispatched to eight different forest fires and, for all of 1936, had more man-hours on fires than any other camp in the state.[23]

Less well known, but nevertheless important, were the special projects and duties performed by California's African-American CCC companies. In many forests, canyons, and parks of the state, African-American companies maintained and helped construct major parks and campground facilities. Most of the CCC camps occupied by African-American companies in California can best be described as multipurpose facilities. Each camp had between two and six project superintendents; each superintendent had a crew assigned to a particular task, such as fire suppression or construction of truck trails and telephone lines. Each camp performed different types of work projects that usually took about three weeks to complete. Routine work done by African-American CCC companies in California included construction and maintenance of park roads, service-truck trails, fire breaks, and hiking trails.

Although some of the African-American camps only did routine work, others were associated with specific projects. Such was the case in an area of the Cleveland National Forest. Working under foreman C. L. Hayes, Company 2923-C of Camp La Cienega gained prominence in fire suppression by using pigeons to transmit messages during fires.[24] According to one former corpsman in the company, "None of the other companies in the district would take on this project. We wanted to be different." The company built the coops, raised the pigeons in the camp, and trained them to fly from fire areas to fire-suppression camps at times when other means of communication were impractical. Company 2923-C was the first company in the United States to use homing pigeons as messengers.[25]

The construction of a telephone line linking the Forest Service line at Descanso with that of the State Division of Forestry at La Mesa, California, was another special project undertaken by an African-American company. This project was started under considerable handicap. The end of the enrollment period six months earlier had left the telephone construction crew of Company 2924-C with only three experienced men and a handful of rookies. Yet the company successfully completed the project, performing all of the work from start to finish, except for surveying.[26]

African-American Company 2925-C both rebuilt and improved Camp Alta Loma and also constructed the Deer Creek Flood Control Dam, located near the small community of Alta Loma, California. The corpsmen worked on the dam for months in winter conditions. The dam, known as the Deer Creek Flood Control Project, improved both recreation facilities and flood protection. The performance of Company 2925-C was also commendable at Camp Kenworthy. Here, J. W. Salle, forestry superintendent, directed the work of constructing the first truck trails on Santa Rosa Mountain and Forbes Ranch, located in the San Bernardino National Forest. In spite of hazardous working conditions, the work of these "trail blazers" was completed without a single reported injury.[27]

African-American CCC companies made major contributions to the development, protection, and maintenance of California's national forests and parks. They completed important campground development and landscaping and removed hazards from miles of roads and trails. They also helped to reduce substantially the forest acreage lost to fires in the state, which led to dramatic savings of timber and property.

3

Camp Life: Education, Recreation, and Community Relations

In May 1933, the Corps began to publish an independent national newspaper called *Happy Days*, a weekly paper that became the official organ of the CCC. Many camps had their own newspapers that were published weekly, semimonthly, or monthly. And, while most of the editors were white, some were African-Americans who made frequent contributions.

Although California had its share of camp newspapers, it was the Los Angeles District *News-Courier* that covered widely the stories and activities of the camps occupied by African-American companies. The *News-Courier* was published semimonthly, and it was "gathered, compiled, and edited by CCC enrollees" in Van Nuys, California.

In September 1936, the staff of the *News-Courier* consisted of thirty-two enrollees: an editor, staff assistant, advertising manager, and twenty-nine camp correspondents from various companies throughout the CCC Los Angeles district. Of this number, three of the correspondents were African-Americans who reported on the activities of the African-American companies. The ten-page paper contained information on camp work projects, sports, poetry, community activities, and general camp news. The few surviving copies of the *News-Courier* are valuable information sources.[1]

Camp life centered around a host of activities, ranging from intercamp sports, such as basketball, baseball, and boxing, to seeking entertainment in neighboring towns. After a hard day's work, recreational and educational activities were a welcome occasion. Once work assignments were completed, the men were allowed to use the remainder of the day as they wished.[2]

After the evening meal, the enrollees were permitted to engage in recreational activities, if they desired. Taking educational courses, watching

movies, letter writing and reading, and just engaging in general conversa-
tion were permitted until 10 P.M., or "lights out." If the camp was located
near a town, the men could, with permission, visit a few nights a week.
They often competed against local sports teams. In the Los Angeles CCC
district, for instance, Company 2923-C, Camp La Cienega, was entertained
by the Federal Music Projects' eight-piece orchestra from Pasadena, California. On Saturdays enrollees were given time to do as they wished, and
many took this "free time" to go into local communities. Some were kept in
camp to assist with the demands of camp operation. During forest fire season, especially during the summer months, sufficient numbers of enrollees
were kept in camp in case of an emergency.[3] Sundays were reserved for
religious services for those who chose to attend church. The ministers, most
of whom were from nearby communities, "preached to the enrollees, coun-
seled them, visited the sick, buried the dead, and performed the few mar-
riages between the men and local women."[4]

On holidays and certain other special occasions, most CCC camps
throughout the nation were given free time to engage in special activities. In
1936 a large contingent of men from Companies 2923-C, Camp La Cienega,
and 2925-C, Camp Alta Loma, were released to participate in the auditions
for prospective vaudeville acts that were to be presented at the San Diego
Exposition. Those who remained at Camp La Cienega, which included most
of the company's drill team, were permitted to perform at the dedication
ceremonies of a new statue at nearby San Diego. On April 4, 1937, "CCC
Day," enrollees were given time off to celebrate. Members of Company 2923-
C celebrated the founding of the Civilian Conservation Corps by staging a
gigantic picnic. The parents, relatives, and friends were invited to attend this
annual affair and to participate in various forms of entertainment, inspection
tours of the camp, and other events of the company.[5]

The Educational Program

The CCC at its inception had no educational program other than the training received on work projects. No reference to an educational program
appears in the original bill establishing the CCC. However, pressure and
support from state selection agencies, educators, President Roosevelt, and
others who were enthusiastic about the educational potential of the CCC
led to the establishment of the Corps Educational Program on May 9, 1933,
five weeks after the president had signed the Emergency Conservation

Work Act, which created the CCC.[6] Director Fechner forwarded an order to all Corps area commanders, which read in part: "Instruction will be given in forestry by members of the Forestry Service and classes in general and vocational educational courses will be conducted, when practicable, by the Army for all members of the Civilian Conservation Corps who so desire it."[7] By June 1934, the CCC Educational Program was operational.

The responsibility for carrying out the educational program was vested in the Department of War, assisted by the Office of Education. Corps area commanders, with the help of a CCC educational adviser, had the responsibility of making sure that the educational program was properly administered. In the Ninth Corps area, John B. Griffing, past president of San Bernardino Junior College in San Bernardino, California, was appointed as the first educational adviser of the Ninth Corps area in January 1934. His principal assignment was supervising the educational work of the educational advisers in each of the CCC camps in the eight western states.[8]

The Corps area educational adviser acted, for the most part, in an advisory capacity. The district educational adviser performed essentially the same function as the district commander. The Committee on Education was composed of the camp commander, educational adviser, project foreman, and, depending upon the camp, sometimes one enrollee.[9]

Yet the educational program was almost entirely in the hands of the camp educational adviser. In addition to providing classroom instruction, the educational adviser was expected to train and supervise other staff members and do a variety of other things necessary to administer a sound educational program. The educational adviser was also required to assist the enrollee with what seemed likely to develop into a "usable skill" once his tenure in the CCC was over. "On-the-job" training included automobile mechanics, carpentry, cabinetmaking, and cooking.[10]

The duties of the educational adviser went far beyond the confines of the camp classroom. As the educational program grew, so did his responsibilities. Courses had to be set up that would meet the needs and interests of the enrollees; instructors had to be recruited to teach the courses; and the monthly educational reports, which were required by the district educational adviser, had to be completed. The adviser also served as a counselor, and when conflicts developed between the enrollees and camp personnel, he often found himself as the mediator.

After the CCC Educational Program was established in late 1933, it soon became apparent that African-Americans would not be appointed as educational advisers, even in racially segregated camps. George F. Zook, then the commissioner of education, and the Corps's education director, C. S. March, had implied early on that "the government intended to appoint white advisers only."[11] However, Secretary of the Interior Harold Ickes encouraged Director Fechner "to appoint blacks to supervisory positions in the CCC."[12] Thus, in May 1934, "fourteen Negroes had received appointments as CCC educational advisers with additional appointments expected later."[13] By September 1935, with the exception of the West Coast, Southeast, and the New England states, African-Americans were being appointed as educational advisers throughout the Corps. In 1940, of the 153 all-African-American companies, all but a few had black educational advisers.[14]

Despite the paucity of direct evidence, it is probable that protests from Edgar C. Brown actually led to the continued appointment of African-Americans to supervisory positions in the Corps. Brown was a relatively unknown journalist who secured a position in the publicity section of the CCC through the recommendation of President Roosevelt. He was able to obtain employment in the Corps as a result of the recommendation of Irvin McDuffie, who was "Roosevelt's valet and Brown's brother-in-law."[15]

Shortly after his appointment to the publicity section of the CCC, Brown became somewhat of an annoyance to CCC administrators in Washington, D.C. Calvin W. Gower, who has written the fullest and only scholarly contribution to the study of blacks' efforts to secure leadership positions in the CCC, has stated that Fechner, in letters to President Roosevelt, noted "that Brown was continually calling the Departments of Agriculture and the Interior complaining about mistreatment of Negroes." "Fechner implied that Brown was partly responsible for the increase in recent months of the agitation for a bigger role in the CCC for Negroes." Fechner concluded, therefore, that Brown should "confine his activities to publicity work on CCC camps for Negro newspapers."[16] President Roosevelt responded: "I agree with you that Brown should confine himself to preparing newspaper material on what Negro C.C.C. camps are doing."[17]

It is unclear whether Brown's minor spot in the CCC actually influenced the Corps' leadership to change its attitude regarding administrative positions for African-Americans; however, it is clear that his efforts did call attention to the need for additional African-American educational advisers.

Lee J. Purnell became the first African-American educational adviser in the California's CCC program. Purnell's name appears throughout the California records of the CCC, but there is little information on his background. One former enrollee recalled that Purnell had been a school-teacher "down south" before going to work for the CCC. In any case, he began his position as educational adviser for Company 2940-C when it was transferred from Camp La Cienega to San Pablo Dam in October 1938. He remained with Company 2923-C until it was disbanded in 1942.[18]

Roy Perry served as educational adviser at Camp Minnewawa. He had taught in a number of high schools in the East and in the Los Angeles school system before going to work for the CCC in June 1936. Before coming to Camp Minnewawa, he was connected with Company 2925-C while it was at Camps Topanga, Alta Loma, Kenworthy, and Piedra Blanca. Perry was by profession a doctor of dental surgery.[19]

In the view of one recruit, Purnell was well liked by both enrollees and the staff. He joked with the enrollees and participated in various camp recreational activities. Roy Perry, on the other hand, while liked by the enrollees, isolated himself. "In the mess hall the head table was for officers and staff. Dr. Perry would eat by himself and not with the officers. It wasn't that he thought he was better than they were, but the impression that he gave me was that he was not as good as they were."[20]

Joshua C. Croom was appointed educational adviser in October 1935. He served as adviser to Company 2922-C at Camp City Creek until it was disbanded three months later. He was then transferred to Company 2923-C, Camp La Cienega, where he remained until May 1936.

William Robinson was assigned as educational adviser for Company 2924-C in June 1936. He remained with the company for approximately seven months.

Herod Ward became educational adviser of Company 2923-C when Croom was relieved, and remained with the company until the summer of 1937, at which time he was transferred to Company 2924-C. He was replaced by Thomas Jackson, who served for nearly two years.[21]

Robert C. Francis became an educational adviser for Company 2923-C in 1940. A former athlete and graduate of the University of California at Berkeley, he remained with Company 2923-C while it occupied Camps Yucca Creek, Marble Fork, and Kaweah in the Sequoia National Park, until the company was disbanded in April 1942.[22]

Each camp educational adviser was required to submit a "CCC Camp Educational Report" once a month. The report filed in February 1941 by Robert Francis, educational adviser at Camp Kaweah in Tulare County, is a typical example. In addition to the basic courses of reading, writing, and arithmetic, ten job training subjects were taught, including auto mechanics, truck driving, carpentry, explosives, welding, cooking and serving, compressor operation, tractor operation, blacksmithing, and pipe laying. Instructors also taught classes in first aid and safety education. The average daily attendance was sixty to eighty enrollees. The results of the month's educational work were said to be as follows: "Education work is steadily improving. The enrollees are evincing growing interest. The courses conducted by the technical service have been done in a creditable manner. However the program is still very inadequate. There is a great need for instructional work that will be accredited by a local high school. No certificates have been issued within the last few months, but in March, a number will be awarded." Subsequent monthly *Educational Reports* reveal that the educational program at Camp Kaweah did not develop further, nor were additional certificates issued to enrollees.[23]

Judging from the available sources on the educational program in California there were few differences in the courses offered in African-American and white CCC camps. However, a noticeable variation in the educational program that deserves mention is the absence in educational reports of any mention of courses in cooking and serving in camps occupied by white corpsmen. All of the camps occupied by African-American recruits offered a course in "serving." What this suggests is that African-American enrollees, unlike whites, were being systematically prepared for what was viewed as traditional "Negro jobs."

The courses offered to the men of 2925-C at Camp Kenworthy were generally vocational in nature. Auto mechanics, carpentry, and cooking were available, as well as classes in electronics and telephone line construction.[24]

Frequently lectures by district chaplains and ministers from the San Diego African-American community were given to the corpsmen of Company 2924-C at Camp Minnewawa. Educational films were shown twice monthly. Business English, U.S. history, and elementary education were also available, as well as courses in typing, journalism, radio operation, and wood carving.[25]

Lee Purnell, educational adviser for Company 2940-C at San Pablo Dam, stressed "practical" vocational courses as part of the educational program. The courses included cooking, typing, auto mechanics, and concrete construction. For those with "higher aspirations," a number of college courses were offered, the most popular being geography and administration.[26]

While most courses were taught by the educational adviser, Army officers and members of the technical staff, occasionally local educators provided classroom instruction for enrollees. The thoroughgoing educational program at Camp Piedra Blanca was due, in part, to the cooperation given Company 2925-C by the Ventura County school system. It was reported that at Camp Piedra Blanca, Company 2925-C had the distinction of being the first African-American camp in the Ninth Corps area to have a full-time schoolteacher.[27]

Frequently, qualified enrollees became part of the teaching staff. Two instructors shared their years of experience with the corpsmen of Company 2925-C while it occupied the Alta Loma facility near the community of Alta Loma, California. One instructor with thirty-five years of experience taught classes in cooking and baking. The other enrollee, with cards of identification from several construction firms, shared his knowledge of electricity and carpentry.[28]

Camp libraries were an important part of the CCC educational program. Most books were purchased from company funds or received as private donations. The library at Camp San Pablo Dam contained 554 volumes, all of which were acquired by donation. At Camp La Cienega the library had two hundred reference volumes, one thousand general works, plus six magazines, two daily newspapers, and three weekly subscriptions. Camp Minnewawa, at Jamul, California, received two African-American weekly newspapers and subscribed to ten daily metropolitan papers. Numerous popular magazines were donated by the citizens of San Diego.[29]

The primary purpose of the CCC educational program was to train the enrollees in a skill with which they might secure employment after discharge. According to CCC records of African-American camps in California, seven members of Company 2923-C received jobs in private industry after leaving Camp La Cienega—four as auto mechanics, two as carpenters' helpers, and one as an electrician. At Camp Pine Valley several men of Company 2924-C found employment in national defense industries, while others became clerks in the Selective Service. In the academic program, African-American enrollees took advantage of the various courses offered. Some were able to make up high school deficiencies, while others enrolled for college credit, and certificates were awarded to corpsmen of Company 2923-C for these achievements.[30]

Employment records of African-American companies in California suggest that the education and training program of the CCC was implemented and carried out successfully. Yet few of the participants interviewed for this study were employed in technical fields after discharge. Most found employment as laborers. Furthermore, oral and written sources reveal that most of the participants denied that the training they received added to their employability. Thus, as one critic of the CCC's educational program concluded, and this can be applied to African-American enrollees in California, it failed "to grasp fully the golden opportunity to develop a thoroughgoing program of remedial education and vocational training leading to eventual re-employment."[31]

The Recreational Program

In order to develop good morale and loyalty, as well as provide goodwill for the CCC in local circles, Camp Commanders provided recreational and entertainment activities as a means of reaching this end. Initially, the junior officers in each camp were responsible for organizing sports and social events. However, with the emergence of the Corps's educational program, the educational adviser took over as recreational director.

Oral sources and press coverage as well as official records testify to the many and varied leisure activities of camps occupied by African-American companies in California. The Federal Music Projects from Pasadena, California, entertained the enrollees of 2923-C, La Cienega, complete with its eight-piece orchestra. Some highlights of the program included renditions of "Sugar Blues," "Hot Lips," and "The Music Goes Round and Round." The next year the camp's chorus, quartet, and orchestra traveled to Riverside, California, to perform for the Riverside American Legion Post. A humorous comment made by the camp's news correspondent stated that the performance would "endeavor to make the members of the Post forget that Gene Austin, Dick Powell, Bing Crosby, Morton Downey or Rudy Vallee ever existed." On several occasions this company had also been asked to present performances by its drama group to local functions. At Camp Minnewawa entertainers from camps located in the southern section of the Los Angeles CCC district got together to prepare for two days of "CCC Day" activities in nearby San Diego. One representative from Company 2925-C, Alta Loma, played the accompaniment for several of the numbers, in addition to giving his interpretation of "My Gal's Good Lookin." Also included in the group of numbers heard were "three colored gentlemen from Camp La Cienega and calling themselves the 'Three Ravens'."[32]

Dances and other social affairs formed an important and necessary part of the CCC recreational program. When Company 2923-C moved to Camp San Pablo Dam in October 1938, the city of Oakland, California, became the choice for recreational activities, due primarily to its large African-American community. One former enrollee remarked that "many of us knew that attending church in Oakland was a good way to meet girls. Since many of the African-American churches had recreational activities for young people, this was a good opportunity to meet local girls and get dates." The community leaders came out to camp, met with staff members, and made arrangements for enrollees to be transported to dances, parties, church activities, social programs, and other forms of recreation and entertainment. The company commander also made arrangements whereby camp trucks were dispatched to Oakland to pick up young ladies who wanted to attend dances, musical revues, and other forms of in-camp entertainment.

When the company was transferred to Camp Yucca Creek in early 1939, the enrollees participated in many district athletic activities as well as some local sports functions in Porterville, California. However, for recreation and entertainment the men chose nearby Fresno—again due to the fact that Fresno had an African-American community. Porterville enjoyed good community-camp relations, and both religious and educational facilities of this community were used.[33]

While stationed at Camp Alta Loma, the members of Company 2925-C chose to bypass the communities of Upland, Cucamonga, Fontana, and Rialto, where few recreational and entertainment facilities were available. Instead, they selected San Bernardino as their recreational community because of its large population, numerous theaters, and other places of recreation and entertainment, and most important—an African-American community that welcomed them.[34]

Movie theaters were always popular. Once every two weeks corpsmen of Company 2925-C would travel to nearby San Bernardino, and once a week to Hemet, California, about twenty-six miles away for motion picture shows. Occasionally they would travel to Los Angeles, approximately 133 miles from camp. On all of these so-called liberty parties, enrollees were accompanied by a "convoy officer" who acted as a police officer.

Another means of maintaining good morale among enrollees was the granting of awards to individuals and recognition to camps. These awards were made on the basis of each camp's cleanliness, discipline, leadership, administration, and productiveness.[35] Enrollee Roy E. Wallace, Company

2923-C, Camp La Cienega, received the *News-Courier*'s written bouquet for meritorious service because of "the perfection of his reports" with the Los Angeles district's Personnel and Record Section. Ocea McNill, an enrollee in Company 2925-C, Camp Kenworthy, was named the best truck driver in the district for the month of August 1936.[36]

Recognition was given to companies judged outstanding on the basis of inspection reports, work projects, and other interesting sidelights. In his "Camp Report" to the national office in Washington, D.C., CCC special investigator M. J. Bowen commented that the black company that occupied Camp San Pablo Dam was "the best Camp of colored boys that I have ever inspected, and will match with some of our best White Camps."[37] Company 2924-C, while at Camp Minnewawa, with its neat barracks and blooming gardens, was well publicized as the Los Angeles district's "Camp of the Flowers," which made it one of the outstanding CCC camps in the district. The same company was praised for its construction and repair of many miles of roadway in almost inaccessible regions, which proved to be beneficial to fire suppression crews and homesteaders who lived in the vicinity of the camp.[38]

Like most CCC camps in California, those occupied by African-Americans organized sports teams as part of the recreational program. Nearly every African-American company camp had basketball and baseball teams that entered local competition with surrounding communities. Company 2923-C, Camp La Cienega, received considerable recognition by playing baseball against various teams in nearby Elsinore, California, and the camp gained a great deal of favorable publicity.[39] During the season the basketball teams competed against various teams in nearby Elsinore, California, with great success. "In Elsinore, we had a reputation of having a good basketball team," recalled an assistant to the camp's educational adviser. "None of the local teams could beat us. We always played harder when there were girls around."[40] Camp San Pablo Dam had an excellent team that entered in one of the numerous leagues in and around the San Francisco Bay Area.[41]

Basketball was the most popular sport among CCC enrollees. With African-American companies in California it was the most widely played. Enrollees participated in both CCC district and local competition.

When Company 2940-C was organized at Camp San Pablo Dam in August 1935, Educational Adviser Lee J. Purnell quickly put together an excellent athletic program. Many of the men participated in boxing, volleyball, baseball, or basketball. The boxing team won every class in the 1936 Spring

Boxing Tournament held at Sacramento CCC district headquarters. That same year the company also won the baseball championship of the district and captured the runner-up cup in the basketball tournament.[42]

CCC enrollees also participated in various intramural activities. Intercamp competition was especially popular in areas away from city limits where recreational activities were somewhat limited. Touch football was popular with competition also available in horseshoes, table tennis, pool, chess, and Chinese checkers.[43]

On the whole, the recreational activities in camps occupied by African-American companies in California were helpful in maintaining good relations among enrollees. In most of the camps the recreational programs were well organized and received excellent ratings from Corps and district inspectors. The enrollees established an enviable record in their conduct and association with both blacks and whites in the surrounding communities in which they engaged.[44] As a collective group, African-American companies were outstanding in sports competition, both team and individual. In district and Corps area competitions, whether basketball, baseball, or boxing, the African-American enrollee or team was usually in the final competition and more often than not the champions. Although sports were less remembered than other facets of the CCC program, the enrollees obviously broadened their horizons through their association with each other, as well as the surrounding communities. Indeed, if the CCC recreational programs had made no other contribution, this alone would have been sufficient justification for its existence.

Community Relations and African-American Companies

In October 1929, on the eve of the "Great Crash," California was an enormous, moderately conservative, ethnically diverse, primarily Anglo-Saxon state. As African-Americans migrated to California in the late 1920s and early 1930s, discrimination became a major problem. Discrimination regarding jobs and housing and the increasing tension between blacks and whites, particularly in the large urban areas where African-American communities were expanding, characterized race relations in California on the eve of the New Deal. The reception given African-American CCC companies by certain localities naturally reflected these relations.

Community acceptance of camps occupied by African-American corpsmen varied throughout the nation. In most cases, communities near CCC camps were close-knit, all-white and openly biased, and did not welcome African-American enrollees. Director Fechner maintained that "there is hardly a locality in this country that looks favorably or even with indifference, on the location of a Negro CCC camp in their vicinity." John A. Salmond noted that white residents "feared the effect of a large body of Negroes on the social stability of their community. They anticipated great increases in drunkenness and other social vices, and in particular, they feared for the safety of white women and children."[45] In most states local resentment toward all-African-American camps was a fundamental problem for CCC officials, and the state of California was no exception.

Unfortunately, extensive sources on the impact of African-American CCC companies and camps on California communities are not available. Not even the press published much information pertaining to African-American camps. But the written and oral sources that are available shed some light on the reaction to African-American corpsmen in many California communities.

During the period of assignment of Company 2923-C to Camp San Pablo Dam, several instances of harassment by white members of the community of Richmond were reported by enrollees. On more than one occasion African-American enrollees, particularly truck drivers who were regularly dispatched to Richmond to accomplish company business, were openly intimidated by police officers. One former CCC official in California recalled an incident involving a Company 2923-C truck driver and a member of the Richmond police force: "On one occasion a police officer told the Company 2923-C truck driver, 'we don't want you damned niggers in our town.' Upon reporting this incident to the commanding officer, the enrollee was instructed to ignore such remarks and just do his duties. On his next trip to Richmond this enrollee and his swamper [assistant] were arrested by the same police officer, who said, 'I just told you damned niggers to stay out of town.' These enrollees were charged with 'vagrancy' and held in the city jail."[46]

As a result of this incident, Captain Kenneth P. Jones, the commanding officer, placed Richmond "off-limits" to all Company 2923-C enrollees. Arrangements were made with the Richmond postmaster to have mail picked up and delivered to the camp.[47]

Company 2924-C, also stationed at the San Pablo Dam facility, was forced to disband as a result of months of harassment from citizens committees from the Richmond community.[48] It also became necessary to place Richmond "off-limits" to Company 2940-C while it was assigned to Camp

San Pablo Dam, from August 1, 1935, to April 10, 1937. Following the necessary coordination with the district commander of the Los Angeles CCC district, the decision was made to transfer all corpsmen remaining on the rolls to Company 2924-C, Camp Minnewawa, a desolate and remote camp located south of San Diego, just a few miles from the Mexican border. According to the camp adjutant serving at the time, the commanding officer, Captain Russell Louden, made the order to disband and transfer known to the enrollees as follows: "At evening retreat, 4–9–37, no announcement was made. At midnight, 4–9-, 10–37, Captain Louden had the Company Clerk ring the fire bell. While all members of the company were reporting to the parade ground in various degrees of dress/undress, putting on fatigues and trying to get in formation, presuming that they were going out on a fire call, Captain Louden was preparing his 'final speech.' 'I'm transferring all of you niggers to Mexico. Now go back to your barracks, pack up, and be ready to leave right after breakfast.'"[49]

Protests were made against 2924-C's occupation of Camp Minnewawa at Jamul, California. The Chamber of Commerce in nearby La Mesa sent a petition to district Congressman George Burham requesting that African-Americans not occupy the camp at Minnewawa. In a letter to Director James McEntee, Special Investigator A. W. Stockman reported that he had "received a message . . . saying a serious situation was developing as a result of the announced occupancy of Minnewawa Camp, Jamul, California, by an all-colored company. The message said 'hell is a popping.'" However, the assistant CCC director's personal investigation showed that due consideration was given to the occupation of Camp Minnewawa by an African-American company, and "it appears that no harm will result therefrom." His investigation concluded that "it has been our experience during the past three years that colored companies have performed good work and have conducted themselves in a proper manner." Although the La Mesa Chamber of Commerce remained opposed to the occupation of Camp Minnewawa by an African-American company, the enrollees remained there despite the series of complaints.[50]

When Company 2923-C left Camp La Cienega in 1938, the intention of district headquarters was to move to a new camp location in Griffith Park in Los Angeles. The city's park commissioners refused to give or lease land in Griffith Park for an African-American CCC company. The reason given was an "old ordinance of the cities of Burbank and Glendale which prohibited Negroes from remaining inside municipal limits after sun down."[51]

Yet many local communities tolerated African-American enrollees and were not hostile to an African-American CCC camp. White citizens of Elsinore, California, for instance, initially resented the idea of an African-American company, but after talking with Camp Minnewawa commander, Captain Ralph C. Williams, "they changed their opinions as they felt that he would keep the situation well in hand, and that nothing would be allowed to disturb the town's civic and social routine." Elsinore's chief of police, other town executives, and several leading businessmen declared that "the colored boys would be welcome and would be shown every ordinary courtesy until any abuse of the privilege might occur." An enrollee who remained in the Elsinore area after his CCC duty was over recalled that "at first the people were suspicious, but soon we were welcome and invited to community functions." In an effort to promote harmony early on, Captain Williams planned a "homecoming" for the corpsmen of Company 2923-C with families and friends, the mayor of Elsinore, community organizations, the police chief, and other notables of the community. And in celebration of the fifth anniversary of the CCC, African-American residents of nearby San Diego attended an open house at Camp Minnewawa where entertainment programs were performed by enrollees.[52]

A possible explanation for Elsinore's tolerance of Company 2923-C is that occasionally camp administrators resided in surrounding communities and frequently participated in social and religious activities. These endeavors often helped to enhance good relations between the CCC and localities.

As some former enrollees have previously indicated, African-American communities in California were receptive to African-American corpsmen. CCC veterans also say that the positive reactions to African-American camps and companies outnumbered negative reactions. A Los Angeles enrollee who worked briefly for Hughes Aircraft after leaving the CCC stated that "I was treated nicely in every respect." "The black neighborhood in San Diego treated enrollees well," according to a former educational adviser for Company 2924-C. Another enrollee, also from Los Angeles, said that "during my first enlistment period relations with black neighborhoods were normal, but we were not permitted to enter the white town of Ojai."[53]

Thus, while African-American California communities accepted the idea of an all-African-American camp located therein or nearby, most white localities remained hostile. Blacks were, as one scholar has noted, "simply not welcome."[54]

CCC officials in California sought to maintain camp discipline as a means of ensuring favorable community relations and respect. Established CCC regulations permitted camp administrators to issue penalties for minor offenses by enrollees. Restrictions of privileges, extra duty, deduction of pay, and dishonorable discharges for extreme offenses were given as punishment. Yet these punitive measures did not entirely deter disturbances in some CCC camps. An enrollee at Camp Minnewawa was arrested in San Diego for stealing an automobile. At Camp La Cienega an enrollee of Company 2923-C staged a one-man riot in protest against the expulsion of three admitted communists. He was sentenced to serve ninety days in the Riverside County Jail. In another instance, members of Company 2925-C, Alta Loma, California, staged a hunger strike because "rice was served for breakfast instead of potatoes" and "a foreman named 'Winchester' was driving and overworking them." Two of the enrollees received dishonorable discharges. Special Investigator Stockman, while irritated by the incident, sought to put the best possible light on its origins: "The unsatisfactory condition of the camp and the restrictions placed upon them, together with the knowledge that they had been forced to leave their former camp as a result of the local public opinion, disheartened and discouraged the enrollees." He also expected reaction from African-American political and subversive circles in Los Angeles, maintaining that "a great part of the trouble in this camp, and possibly other camps (colored) can be attributed to these sources."[55]

Rebellion against authority in the CCC camps occupied by African-Americans was, for the most part, limited to a small number of individuals. A detailed investigation by the national office in Washington, D.C., usually followed an incident to determine who was responsible and what steps were necessary to prevent disturbances from recurring. These efforts were essential not only for maintaining cordial relations between the camps and the nearby communities, but a necessary measure for upholding the reputation of the entire CCC program.

4

African-Americans in California's CCC

Although the CCC officially came to an end in 1942, its impact continued in several respects. One way was through the tangible Corps achievement of its principal task, "conservation." Unquestionably, the CCC made important contributions to the maintenance of California's natural resources. Major accomplishments included 30,766,050 trees planted; 307 lookout towers constructed; 8,704 miles of telephone lines laid; 1,161,921 miles of truck trails and minor roads created; and thousands of acres of land saved from the ravages of disease, fire, and soil erosion. Numerous parks and recreation areas were entirely built or improved by the CCC. Mt. Tamalpais, Muir Woods National Monument, Prairie Creek Redwoods State Park, Morro Bay, Calaveras Big Trees State Park, as well as Yosemite National Park, Sequoia National Park, and Lassen Volcanic National Park were all significantly improved with CCC labor.[1] The fact that African-American corpsmen participated fully in the conservation of the state's natural resources deserves to be recorded in CCC history.

Any discussion of the value of the CCC to California must give some attention to the economic effect the program had on the state. In California, 135,401 men were employed by or enrolled in the CCC during the years 1933–1942. According to the Department of Forests and Parks (the state forester and the state park director were asked to submit a biennial report on CCC activities), the CCC spent a total of $154,545,757 during the nine years of the program—far greater than the totals for other states in the Ninth Corps area.[2]

It was estimated that approximately $25,643,910 in monthly allotments went to parents of the 120,063 enrollees from California. The $300 per year that was returned to an enrollee's family was not impressive by contemporary standards; but in a period of mass unemployment such an amount was much to be desired.

The Civilian Conservation Corps's policy of racial segregation was obviously discriminatory and racially motivated. Yet this was not without some measurable benefits. Coincident with the establishment of all-African-American companies, African-American enrollees in California were for the first time able to assume positions of leadership, both administrative and technical, in addition to the work projects, which ranged from training pigeons and managing a wild elk herd to constructing large concrete dams and steel suspension bridges. Because of discrimination in predominantly white CCC companies, such a demonstration was hardly possible in an integrated setting.

I do not mean to imply or suggest that the opportunity to assume these subpolicy positions established camp segregation as a positive good for African-Americans in the CCC. The matter is more complex. What is suggested is that given the available options, combined with the ambivalent racial policy of New Dealers, the unsympathetic attitude of the CCC director and the Army regarding leadership matters, and certainly national public opinion on racial issues in the 1930s, the segregation of the races and consequent appointment of African-Americans to supervisory positions was a maximal response to the hard reality of race relations nationwide. Indeed, as skimpy as the African-Americans' share of leadership positions might have been, it was as one scholar has put it, "more than blacks were accustomed to getting."[3]

Although a few supervisory positions were staffed by African-Americans in California's CCC, no African-Americans served in policy-making positions. There were, as mentioned, no African-American commanders for the five African-American companies established in the state; nor were African-American reserve officers, medical officers, or chaplains called for duty with the CCC. To use African-American officers, the War Department believed, would "result in negro enrollees getting out of hand and precipitating a situation which would be inevitably worse in every way than any reaction that might result from the non-employment of colored Reserve Officers." Thus, there was no attempt made by CCC officials in California to challenge the racial status quo.[4]

The CCC in California had other objectionable features. While there was some attempt to reach a proportionate share of African-American youth in the program, particularly in the later years of the CCC, as illustrated in the table on page 62,[5] they were not enrolled according to need; and when

Table 4.1. African-American CCC Enrollment Applications in the Ninth Corps Area[a]

Enrollment Period	Number Applied	Number Enrolled	Percentage
January 1940	222	52	23.4
April 1940	478	203	42.5
July 1940	232	151	65.1
October 1940	299	127	42.5
January 1941	178	164	92.1
April 1941	205	192	93.7

[a]Data compiled from a memorandum to W. Frank Persons from Neal Guy (April 7, 1941), who estimated that California provided 98 percent of the Ninth Corps Area African-American enrollees. With the exception of April and October 1940, the increase in the number of acceptable African-American enrollees in California's CCC can best be explained by the low enrollment of whites who were finding employment opportunities in the state's defense industry.

admitted, they were often subjected to segregation and open hostility within the Corps and from nearby white communities.

Despite discrimination against African-American corpsmen in California, the hopes, spirits, the very lives of African-American youth were conserved. It gave them a place in the economic and social world at a time when hundreds of thousands of young people in California, and America in general, were caught in a sea of apathy and hopelessness. Indeed the CCC gave these young men not only food, clothing, housing, and educational and recreational opportunities, but also provided vital assistance to their families.

On June 6, 1935, President Roosevelt expanded his effort to help youth by signing into law the National Youth Administration (NYA). The NYA, directed by Aubrey Williams, was established primarily to complement and extend the work of the CCC in alleviating the problems of unemployed youth. The major purposes of the NYA were to provide financial assistance to needy high school and college students, which would enable them to complete their formal education, and to give job training to those young people who had left school and were unemployed.[6]

In the NYA, African-Americans were enrolled according to need and not, as in the case of the CCC, simply as part of the general population. In July 1936 a special Division of Negro Affairs was established as an integrated part of the national organization and directed by Mary McLeod

Bethune, a prominent African-American educator.[7] The Division of Negro Affairs attempted to ensure adequate integration of the black viewpoint in planning, as well as the day-by-day operations.[8] This division participated fully in the policy at the national, state, and local levels.[9] Indeed, the status of Bethune contributed to the prestige of the division and helped to ensure that African-American youth became eligible for NYA funded programs. Therefore, unlike the CCC, where limitations on African-American participation was the practice, the NYA paid particular attention to the problems of African-American youth in an effort to redress the imbalances started and maintained by the Corps.[10]

The CCC in California: As African-American Participants Saw It

Five years after the establishment of the CCC, President Roosevelt summarized the accomplishments of the Corps:

> When in 1933 I asked the Congress to provide for the Civilian Conservation Corps I was convinced that forest lands offered one source for worthwhile work . . . for large numbers of our unemployed. Events of the past five years have indicated that my earlier conviction was well founded. In rebuilding and managing those lands, and in the many uses of them and their resources, there exists a major opportunity for new employment and for increasing the national wealth.[11]

The question of perceivable benefits is perhaps better told by the CCC participants than by anyone else. The benefits varied for individuals, but they applied to primarily three areas: employment, training, and character development.

Employment

From the beginning of the program, providing employment for needy youth was recognized and emphasized by the Corps. The immediate value of employment is seen clearly when former enrollees were queried on the reasons why they joined the CCC. An enrollee who was a squad leader remarked: "This was during an extreme depression in the country. No jobs were available and the money was needed to help support my mother." A former truck operator recalls that "jobs were scarce at the time and the Three C's . . . helped my family in Fresno who needed it." "Times were extremely hard in California," declared an ex-Oklahoman, "and jobs were hard to find. I just had to have a job." A former dynamite handler commented, "I joined because of a lack of jobs . . . one could earn his way."[12]

Although most of the former enrollees considered employment in the CCC to be of help to them and their families, the Corps' employment was, in fact, always of immediate, if not always lasting, value. The following comments are representative of those who felt that the Corps did not prepare them for their lifetime vocation. An enrollee who was assigned to kitchen duty recalled that after leaving the CCC, "I worked in a laundry starching shirts . . . the CCC experience did not apply." An enrollee with four years of service commented: "I was a cook before I went into the CCC and being a cook in the Three C's was just another job." A retired construction worker and packinghouse employee in Los Angeles felt that "the CCC did not help me at all when I looked for a job. . . . In fact, I didn't expect the work in the CCC to prepare me for employment once my CCC duty was over." Another enrollee assigned to kitchen duties in the Corps and who held such jobs as dishwasher, cotton picker, and waiter when discharged noted that "I didn't learn anything that benefited me when I got out of the CCC. . . . I can say that the CCC in no way helped me to get a job." "The CCC did not prepare me for future employment," declared a former police detective with the Los Angeles Police Department.[13]

Many of the work projects of the CCC required only the simplest types of common labor; yet most of the former enrollees did admit that they learned how to cooperate with fellow workers and supervisors, the proper care of equipment, and the importance of hard work and a responsible attitude toward a job.

Although some of the individuals in this study considered their employment in the Corps of little lasting value, others spoke of the CCC as having been a valuable asset in later years. One former enrollee who learned to operate a truck in the CCC maintained that his experience as a driver was extremely important when he applied for a position with the City of Los Angeles in 1939. He recalled that "when I received a recommendation from my camp commander . . . and presented it to the City, I was hired." Another former truck operator in the Corps, who also applied for a position with the City of Los Angeles upon discharge, commented on his work assignment as a driver. In all respects, his experience prepared him for "a job driving a heavy duty truck with the City of Los Angeles for thirty-three years." He also pointed out that his experience as a truck operator was responsible for his assignment as a vehicle operator in the Army during World War II. A former teacher in San Diego felt that his assignment as "an assistant to the Educational Advisor and a clerk in the Forestry Office was immensely beneficial when I was a student at San Diego Junior College."[14]

Though opinions were mixed concerning the CCC's value relative to "worthwhile" employment, most of the former enrollees considered their work experiences to be valuable not only because of their financial benefits, but also because of the attitudes and work habits that were enhanced.

Training

As indicated earlier, the CCC program provided a type of formal education that was conducted during off-duty hours on a strictly voluntary basis. The general purpose of the educational program was to enable the participant to improve himself so that he might be more employable once his service in the Corps was over. While many of the former enrollees considered the courses of instruction to be informative, they were, in essence, of little benefit on a long-term basis. In fact, of the persons whom I was able to contact who had taken courses, only one ex-enrollee thought that the CCC educational program had any lasting value. He considered courses in conservation, photography, and especially library administration to be of considerable value when he applied for a position in the San Diego school system. The value of the educational plan was, however, not equally beneficial for all of the enrollees. Another former enrollee maintained that while he enjoyed the course in radio operation, it was of little value as far as developing skills necessary for entrance into the job market. In the opinion of another enrollee who enrolled in such courses as law, public speaking, and American history, "they were informative and enjoyable . . . , but how many Negroes in the 1930s got jobs in public speaking and law?" A former first aid student remarked: "The course in first aid training did very little for me as far as providing a skill. I never expected it to be."[15]

Although the educational program proved less than successful in the preparation of the enrollees future life's work, most indicated their approval of the program because it afforded "special knowledge," which to some was unavailable before.

Character Development

More important than the occupational and educational benefits to which the former enrollees testified were the activities that influenced character development, that is, discipline, maturity, the ability to get along and cooperate with others, and the various recreational activities that taught lessons of teamwork and good sportsmanship. The following remarks are those of respondents who were questioned on the value of the CCC and, in fact, represent a consensus opinion. A former truck driver at Camp Piedra Blanca commented: "It was a chance to grow up and helped much in later life." A mess sergeant with four years in the Corps recalled: "The CCC was a good place to be in the 1930s. . . . It taught me discipline and how to get along with others." Still another truck driver felt that his service in the CCC "was definitely responsible for my career, having taught me discipline and the incentive to try different things." An enrollee who performed a variety of tasks in the Corps recalled that his experience as a firefighter taught him "what real danger was. . . . It also helped me to mature and how to cooperate and get along with others." A former KP (kitchen police) worker remarked: "I enjoyed the CCC because it taught me discipline, self-reliance, maturity, and quite a few other things that I wouldn't have known otherwise."[16]

It was the sense of responsibility, how to associate and cooperate with others from different backgrounds on a common ground, and the value of discipline that seemed to have been so clearly evident among the benefits the enrollees obtained from the CCC. As a program of practical education the CCC was a failure because it provided no new skills that enabled the enrollee to function more effectively in his community. As an agency devoted to fostering future vocational preparedness, its success was less than satisfactory; however, as a builder of character, the Corps was successful in that period of history.

Although the CCC was aimed at the worst aspects of the Depression, it was never more than a short-term and inadequate solution. Why then did this government agency, with no adequate or sufficient response for problems of youth in Depression-era America, seemingly become so popular with former enrollees in California? Despite the segregation on the part of the Corps, most of the participants interviewed were impressed with the CCC. Why were these men so appreciative to this government agency that deviated little from the discriminatory practices of the past?

A number of reasons can be suggested. In the first place, the difficulties of the Depression were severe for white American youth. For African-American youth in the 1930s the problems were intensified because traditional racial practices emerged and worked to their particular disadvantage. Since African-Americans were quite often in dire economic straits and constituted so large a percentage of the unemployed youth population who were on relief, the direct benefits of the CCC were most attractive to those who would receive the benefits—the enrollees and their families.

Second, and equally important, the CCC taught them discipline and how to live and work with others. As one former enrollee at Camp Piedra Blanca noted: "I didn't know of anyone who got a dishonorable discharge, because we all wanted to be in the CCC."[17]

Again, testimonials received from the participants themselves best explain why most of them looked on the Corps with such favorable eyes. An enrollee who was in the CCC from July 1934 to July 1935 at Camp Digger Butte, near Manton, California, stated: "The CCC taught me to be patient. Everything wasn't black and white, but cut and dry. The various sports activities such as basketball and baseball against other fellows and local communities taught me good sportsmanship." Another enrollee who worked in the forestry office at Camp La Cienega said, "I really needed help. . . . I was in junior college at the time. . . . My family needed the money and the CCC was a great help." "I really needed a job making money because jobs were scarce," wrote an enrollee stationed at Camps Bouquet Canyon and Piedra Blanca. "My service in the CCC was extremely educational. I met all kinds of people." An enrollee from a family of fifteen stated: "I really needed a job at the time. My $25 from the CCC went to my mother and she used every bit of it. The CCC was a good thing." "When I joined the Three C's in 1935," declared a firefighter at Camp San Pablo Dam, "times were really hard here in Los Angeles; I had no money and no job. The Three C's gave me food, clothing and shelter. The CCC was great."[18]

By and large, former corpsmen's only complaints concerned the occasional derogatory racial jokes and remarks made by Army officers and forest service personnel. One enrollee recalled that at Camp Piedra Blanca the Army chaplain "told a racist joke and called one enrollee a 'nigger'; but the Chaplain cried and apologized." Another enrollee who served in the Sequoia National Forest noted that on one occasion an Army officer from Texas "jokingly" referred to him as "nigger boy." "At Camp Bouquet Canyon blacks were subjected to numerous racial remarks," stated an enrollee from Los Angeles. In every case, however, the enrollees felt that despite the occasional racial slurs, the Corps was a good experience. "We had some good officers as well as a few who were not so good."[19]

As far as what segregation meant to the former enrollees, there were differences of opinion. Some disliked it altogether, while others thought it was best for all concerned. One enrollee who served at various camps throughout California remarked that at Camp Tuna Canyon, "blacks were put in a separate barracks. This camp was very desirable." "I never liked segregation," explained a Louisiana native. "Everything in America was segregated, so it wasn't any different in the CCC." An enrollee who served briefly in Utah stated that blacks were assigned to one barracks and whites to another. "We didn't like being segregated, but we expected that sort of thing in Utah." "After I got out of the CCC I couldn't understand why they segregated," remarked an enrollee who joined the Corps in July 1934. "At the time it didn't bother me because I had put my CCC experience behind."[20]

Another individual who served in the Corps before enrollees were assigned to companies without regard to color indicated that he was "surprised to hear of segregation in the CCC. I can't understand the need for it. . . . I lived and socialized with whites and so did other blacks."[21]

The Enrollees: The Later Years

The long-term impact of the CCC experience on African-American corpsmen in California turns out to have been significant, making it possible for a relatively small group of young African-Americans, undereducated, jobless, without marketable skills or social credentials, to gain access to mainstream American society, and thus to attain middle-class status.

It is impossible to say definitely whether the former enrollees would have fared as well had they not joined the CCC. However, it is possible to say that the Corps permitted a cadre of African-American youths to develop a strong sense of self-reliance, discipline, confidence, and in some cases job experience. The program's long-range impact can also be traced through the lifestyles that are commonly associated with the middle class—full-time employment, home ownership, and educational attainment, to mention but a few. The lasting benefits of the CCC on many of the African-American participants in California are evident in their lives since the CCC days of 1933–1942. (All of the former enrollees used in this study are retired. Most are homeowners whose children have been college educated.)

After his CCC experience, William Nelson, Company 992, Sequoia National Forest, worked as a truck operator for twenty-five years with the city of Los Angeles. He owned two homes—one in Fresno and the other in Los Angeles, where he lives with his wife. The Nelsons have three children, all of whom have attended college.

Walter Jacobs was a member of Camp Piedra Blanca, Company 2823-C, located near Wheeler Springs, California. After four years in the CCC he obtained a job as a cook with the Southern Pacific Railroad, as a result of his CCC experience. After a brief time with Southern Pacific, he went to work for Amtrak, where he remained for thirty-eight years until his retirement in 1978.

Algy Landry, Camp Juncal, Santa Barbara, California, enlisted in the CCC in June 1934. He was appointed squad leader of twelve men who fought forest fires and built fire breaks. He was honorably discharged in 1935, after a year in the Corps, returning to his hometown of Los Angeles. Unable to find employment, he returned to high school where he completed requirements for graduation. He served in the Los Angeles Police Department as a homicide detective until his retirement in 1980. Landry and his wife have one daughter who, at the time of the interview, was in Navy intelligence at the Pentagon in Washington, D.C.

Norman Moore enrolled in the CCC in Los Angeles, California, in July 1934, at the age of eighteen, upon his graduation from high school. He was assigned to Camp Digger Butte in the Lassen National Forest and stayed one year. When he left the Corps in 1935, he went to work for North American Aviation as a tool and die specialist for thirty-seven years, before retiring in 1979.[22]

Claude Pierce of Los Angeles, California, was enrolled in October 1937 and was assigned to a spike camp with Company 2925-C at Wheeler Springs, California. After leaving the Corps in 1939 he worked briefly as a custodian before entering the Army in 1942. Upon discharge in 1946, he went to work as a truck operator for the city of Los Angeles because of his training in the CCC. He retired after thirty-three years of service.

Robert D'Hue was a CCC educational assistant at Camps San Pablo Dam and La Cienega. After two years in the Corps, he returned to San Diego, California, where he was employed by the defense industry before being drafted into the Army. After completing military service, he returned to San Diego, completed his college education, and eventually accepted a teaching position in the San Diego school district. D'Hue has two children; one, at the time of the interview, was a student at San Diego City College.[23]

Offutt T. MacWilliams was a CCC educational instructor for Company 2924-C at Camp Minnewawa. He formerly resided in Newton, Kansas, where he completed his high school and college work. After his discharge from the CCC in 1942, he was employed by the San Diego County Probation Department, where he remained for twenty-five years.[24]

Willie Stovall started his CCC experience in 1935 at Salt Lake City, Utah, as part of Company 1941. From there he was transferred to Camp San Pablo Dam, Company 2923-C, at Richmond, California, where he worked in the construction of roads and fire trails. After leaving the CCC in 1937, he was employed as a construction worker and a meat packer.

Orlando Coons joined the Corps in 1933 in San Diego, California. He was assigned to Camps Minnewawa and San Pablo Dam. Upon his discharge he returned to San Diego to attend San Diego State University, where he received the B.S. degree in engineering. The Coons have four children, all of whom are college graduates.[25]

Louis T. Shores enrolled in the CCC in Los Angeles, California, in July 1934. He was assigned to Camp Digger Butte, Company 975, in the Lassen National Forest. After one year in the Corps he returned to Los Angeles and was employed as an aircraft assembler for Lockheed Aircraft Corporation in Burbank, California.[26]

As a point of comparison with other blacks similar in age and origin in California, the participants' own testimonies are a reasonable indication that they fared better economically. One enrollee noted that although he would like to have done better financially, "I did fairly well since leaving the CCC. Some of my friends did better, but the majority of them didn't do as well. Most of my friends don't own their own homes." Another enrollee who purchased his first home in 1951 stated that "those who did better worked for the Postal Service. The others didn't seem to do as well." "Most of my friends who were better off worked at the post office, but that wasn't many," recalled a CCC veteran from Los Angeles. A retired truck driver remembered friends who joined the Corps, as well as those who did not: "Most of my friends who didn't get into the Three C's went to work in factories. Four joined the CCC and when they were discharged one became a reporter for the Los Angeles *Sentinel*; one was hired by the Los Angeles Police Department; another became a fireman; and the other retired as a mail carrier. As far as I can recall, two owned their own homes." The spouse of an enrollee who worked for Lockheed Aircraft after receiving an honorable discharge from CCC remembered: "Some blacks were better off [economically], others were not."[27]

To the degree that the CCC benefited the former enrollees as determined by their subsequent careers, it should be apparent that the program did have the rehabilitative effect, at least in California, that is commonly associated with the Corps and its work. Although the CCC failed to provide the enrollees with the specific skills necessary to function effectively in a changing world, it did, however, succeed in helping the former corpsmen develop healthy attitudes, renewed spirits, self-esteem, and the ability to get along and cooperate with their neighbors and fellow countrymen.

But one needs to recognize that the Civilian Conservation Corps' performance with regard to African-American enrollees in California was, in a sense, a diversion from what was really needed to overcome the youth problem in general. Although the CCC certainly provided desperately needed employment to African-American youth, it was a short-term and insufficient solution. The enrollees largely worked in an artificial atmosphere at assignments, such as tree planting, erosion control, and forest development, all impractical experiences given the fact that the majority of the enrollees were from urban areas. The enrollee was, as one scholar of the CCC noted, "discharged to his home community physically greatly improved, probably more alert mentally, but with no new skills which would enable him to function more effectively in that community."[28]

5

Epilogue

The Civilian Conservation Corps left a generally favorable impression on the enrollees encountered in this study. Though the Corps in California did not fully meet even its legal obligations toward African-American enrollees, its immediate results could be seen in employment, training, and social development. The CCC did provide valuable assistance for African-American youth in the state, and many of those interviewed suggested that a program similar to the original Corps be instituted in current times. The following remarks are representative of proponents of such a program. A former enrollee from Los Angeles who served briefly in Oregon commented: "I would be in favor of a new CCC. . . . It would take many boys off the street." A former corpsman at Camp Juncal near Santa Barbara wrote: "It would be a panacea for high school dropouts and an excellent way to keep youngsters off the streets that are unable to find employment—plus teaching them discipline." Another ex-enrollee felt that "a new CCC would be a great help to young people, especially those who don't have jobs. I would definitely be in favor of it." "Yes, all boys completing high school should enroll in this service or at least spend a year in the Army," remarked a native of New Orleans, Louisiana. A former assistant educational adviser at Camp La Cienega stated: "I think that a program like the CCC would be a great benefit to the youth of today."[1]

Efforts to revive a CCC-type organization at the national level have not been successful. However, efforts have been realized in California and Wisconsin, where conservation programs have been established to put young people to work in the state's parks and public lands. The California Conservation Corps (CCC) and the Wisconsin Conservation Corps (WCC) are coeducational, unlike their predecessor, the Civilian Conservation Corps.[2]

The California Conservation Corps and Wisconsin Conservation Corps: Reviving an Idea

With social conditions today similar for many young people to those of the 1930s, especially for many African-American teenagers who are out of work, it is useful to examine the California Conservation Corps (CCC) and the Wisconsin Conservation Corps (WCC) to see how both programs operate and their accomplishments to date.

The California Conservation Corps' work is, in general, similar to that performed by the original CCC. The contemporary CCC grew out of the Ecology Corps established by Governor Ronald Reagan in 1971. In July 1979, the California Conservation Corps was established by Governor Jerry Brown. It was renewed on a short-term basis until 1983, when Governor George Deukmejian approved legislation making the CCC a permanent department. Corpsmembers must be between the ages of eighteen and twenty-five and not on parole or probation. They represent a cross-section of California youth—urban and rural, high school dropouts and college students, representatives of all ethnic groups.[3]

To date, the California Conservation Corps has planted millions of trees, constructed thousands of miles of trails, and provided countless hours of public service conservation work and emergency assistance to the state of California. Corpsmembers also have an opportunity to pursue educational or vocational goals. Those who are high school graduates or who have taken some college or university courses can earn college credits, with tuition paid by the CCC. Those who haven't completed high school take the courses they need for a GED or diploma. Evening classes are taught by local high school or community college instructors.[4]

CCC enrollees take advantage of the numerous classes that emphasize work values, careers, and job-seeking techniques. They also learn how to complete a job application, write a resume, and participate in mock interviews.

When the Wisconsin Conservation Corps was established in 1983, "the Civilian Conservation Corps of the 1930s served as a model." Corps members must be unemployed young adults ages eighteen to twenty-five. In addition to learning techniques in natural resource conservation, WCC participants also build handicap-accessible ramps, playgrounds, and they remodel, landscape, and weatherize schools and community centers. Corps members who successfully complete the program are eligible for college tuition vouchers of $2,600.[5]

The Debate Continues

The success of the original CCC and the more recent California Conservation Corps and Wisconsin Conservation Corps deserves a closer look as policymakers consider effective approaches to the reduction of youth unemployment. Many oppose revival of the CCC or a similar national program on the grounds that similar national programs, now defunct, were not effective. Few works critical of programs designed to help unemployed young people, in general, and the poor in particular, have received more attention than Charles Murray's *Losing Ground: American Social Policy, 1950–1980.* The book is a vehement attack on the welfare state and those who support it. Murray considers the Great Society of the mid-1960s and many of its programs to be unworkable and counterproductive. He discusses the unsatisfactory results of various job training and community action programs designed to eliminate poverty. Many of the programs, according to Murray, were poorly managed and did little or nothing to help the poor and thus should be eliminated.[6]

A large defect of Murray's attack on the efforts of the state and its assistance to the poor is that he completely ignores those large programs such as the California Conservation Corps, which is apparently so successful that more than forty states and fourteen foreign countries have either visited or contacted it.[7] Any program that not only pays for itself but may also substantially reduce youth unemployment is one that policymakers cannot afford to ignore. If Murray's assumptions about the welfare state imply that nothing can be done for the poor, it is well to remember the Civilian Conservation Corps, an example of a successful effort by the government.

Published reaction to *Losing Ground* has been critical. Robert Greenstein, who in 1985 was director of the Center on Budget and Policy Priorities in Washington, D.C., contends that Murray's book, "with its endless recital of statistics, actually rests on deceptive numbers juggling," and that Murray "consistently omitted or concealed critical facts and research findings that do not support his case." Citing specific examples, Greenstein continues: "Another key element of the Murray thesis is that between 1965 and 1980, when social programs grew, the proportion of black men in the labor force declined and the employment gap between young white men and young black men widened. Once again, according to Murray, the programs were the culprits. Murray produces little evidence of a causal connection. And here, too, the research points largely in other directions." Indeed, Greenstein concludes, "*Losing Ground* is more of a polemical tract than an attempt to examine the complexities and discern the truth about some of the most significant social problems of our times."[8]

To be sure, government programs to help the poor have always had critics. Most observers of policy issues and American government accepted the fact that particular programs often succumb to waste, abuse, and sometimes fraud. Yet, there are the successful programs that have improved the lives of America's poor. In *America's Hidden Success: A Reassessment of the Twenty Years of Public Policy*, published in 1983, John E. Schwartz addressed the debate over whether particular programs curtail the incentive to work. Fifty years after President Roosevelt's New Deal, Schwartz wrote:

> The economic experience of the 1960s and 1970s equally belies a second familiar belief, that is, that welfare programs substantially reduce the incentive to work. True, some effect is possible; it is most likely to be experienced by those Americans who remain at or near the poverty level even when holding down full-time jobs. Nevertheless, neither the expansion of the poverty programs in the 1960s and 1970s, nor the decisive contribution they made to reducing poverty, seems to have come at the cost of much reduction in the incentive of Americans to become a part of the work force and earn a living. . . .
> To help set the context, consider that the numbers of people seeking work and taking jobs increased at historically high rates during these years, by thirty-five percent in 1965–80 alone. Employment climbed at [a] far faster pace during and after the great acceleration of the poverty and welfare programs in 1965–80 than during the preceding fifteen-year period.[9]

Sar Levitan of the Center for Social Policy Studies agreed in 1986 that while there had been some achievements in the welfare system, federal social welfare policy had failed to gain universal acceptance. "In recent years," he wrote, "critics have sought to link rising incidences of crime, drug abuse, divorce, and other social ills with federal social welfare interventions." "Yet a balanced and objective analysis," he insisted, "would reveal that reports of a welfare crisis are greatly exaggerated. Removed from the distortions of budget battles and political ideologies, the record of federal social welfare interventions suggests that the system is a rational and necessary response to emerging societal needs."[10]

In August 1993, 58 Republicans joined 275 Democrats in voting for President Bill Clinton's new National Service program, the National and Community Service Trust Act. The act, which took effect in May 1994, granted awards to individuals seventeen years of age or older who perform service before, during, or after college. The program, Americorps, offers jobs in health care, crime prevention, education, conservation, and other areas of need. Existing federal service programs merged into a new government entity, the Corporation for National and Community Service.

One of the service programs, the Public Lands Corps, is reminiscent of the original CCC. Public Land Corps addresses environmental needs by requiring participants to carry out conservation, restoration, and rehabilitation projects on federal lands, such as fire fighting, trail construction, tree planting, erosion control, and historic preservation. Such work, it is hoped, will provide young people with an appreciation for America's natural and cultural heritage.[11]

The Civilian Conservation Corps in California did provide some useful and important benefits, as the former enrollees have testified. Yet historical judgment of the CCC requires both attention to successes and awareness of its limits. To scholars of the Depression years, the Corps was highly successful in that it contributed to the nation's economic recovery and employed a large percentage of its youthful poor. To these scholars, although the African-American enrollee did not gain the measure of relief to which his economic plight warranted, he was admitted into the CCC. One scholar has noted that the "CCC opened up new vistas for most black enrollees." Leslie Lacy put it clearly: "It usually fed them better than before, provided better living conditions, and gave them valuable academic and vocational training."[12]

There is evidence to support the view that African-Americans did receive some tangible benefits from the CCC experience, at least in the state of California. As some of the former participants have testified, the Corps not only provided short-term employment, but also furnished them with food, clothing, recreation, and marginal educational opportunities.

Available evidence also indicates that the CCC had two programs: one for African-Americans and one for whites. This dichotomy was clearly inconsistent with the rather extraordinary provision attached to the act establishing the CCC, which prohibited discrimination based on race. The Corps's camp segregation policy, however, was consistent with a "separate but equal" policy and perhaps the wording of the provision might have been understood by both black and white to satisfy the requirement of equality at the time. As John L. Saalberg noted in 1962, "segregation was an accepted fact of life, one which the CCC decided to live."[13]

Thus, after 1935, African-American corpsmen lived and worked in all-African-American camps. Although practice varied somewhat, it is clear that African-American corpsmen in California's CCC were treated no differently from African-American enrollees south of the Mason-Dixon Line, contrary to what is seemingly implied in contemporary New Deal scholarship.

Although the CCC was perhaps the best received and certainly the most popular of all the New Deal relief agencies, there is no conclusive evidence that the benefits of the Corps was of any considerable value to African-American enrollees nationally. What is needed are follow-up studies of former enrollees' careers at the state level to determine whether participation in the CCC greatly benefited them.

Conclusion

The Civilian Conservation Corps was an enormous undertaking under very difficult circumstances. It did not solve all of the problems of the jobless young; nor is there evidence that it brought about any measure of change in race relations. The New Dealers did not expect it to. "Those intent upon reforming race relations in the 1930s," Harvard Sitkoff has concluded, "had no tabula rasa upon which to work. They were in the midst of the worst depression in the nation's history."[14] Yet the CCC was, Leslie Lacy has concluded, "the first genuine effort by an American government to undertake, on a massive scale, a basically practical and ideological program for its dispossessed youth."[15]

As a precedent, the image of the CCC is clear: it served as a basis for President John F. Kennedy's Peace Corps in the 1960s, as well as President Lyndon B. Johnson's Job Corps and similar "Great Society" programs. Indeed the permanent testimony of the CCC and its work is the ability of the state to implement reform. The magnitude of the despair and hopelessness of the 1930s required state intervention, and the establishment of the CCC represented the national states' response to the problems of youth. If the Civilian Conservation Corps represented an example of what the government can do for its jobless youth in times of depression, it is certainly worth the effort to put the New Deal to contemporary purposes.

Appendixes

APPENDIX A

Table A.1. Administrative System of the Civilian Conservation Corps

Bold lines indicate major changes in organization and operation.

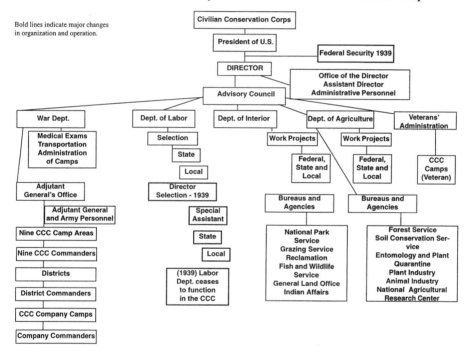

APPENDIX B

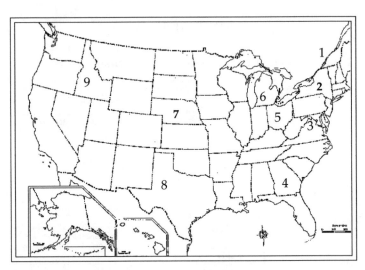

Fig. B.1. Army Corps Area

First	Maine, New Hampshire, Vermont, Massachusetts, Rhode Island, Connecticut
Second	New York, New Jersey, Delaware
Third	Pennsylvania, Maryland, Virginia
Fourth	North Carolina, South Carolina, Tennessee, Mississippi, Louisiana, Alabama, Georgia, Florida
Fifth	Indiana, Ohio, West Virginia, Kentucky
Sixth	Wisconsin, Michigan, Illinois
Seventh	Missouri, North Dakota, South Dakota, Nebraska, Kansas, Minnesota, Iowa, Arkansas
Eighth	Oklahoma, Texas, New Mexico, Colorado, Arizona
Ninth	Montana, Idaho, Wyoming, Utah, Nevada, California, Oregon, Washington

Note: Alaska and Hawaii, which did not achieve statehood until 1959, were not part of the Army Corps area.

APPENDIX C

Table C.1. CCC Camps in California Occupied by Black Companies, 1933–1942

California Camp	Camp Name	Post Office
F-164	La Cienega	Elsinore
NP-5	Yucca Creek	Kaweah
NP-2	Marble Fork	Marble Fork
NP-24	Pinnacles	Pinnacles
F-160	Pine Valley	Pine Valley
F-140	Castaic	Sangus
P-233	Minnewawa	Jamul
P-364	Whitewater	Jamul
P-295	Topanga Canyon	Conoga Park
F-240	Alta Loma	Alta Loma
F-144	Kenworthy	Highland
F-364	Piedra Blanca	Highland
F-157	City-Creek	Highland
SP-7	San Pablo Dam	Richmond

Source: "Location and Strength of Civilian Conservation Corps Projects and Work Companies in the Ninth Corps Area on November 30, 1941," pp. 2–5; CCC Form No. 6. National Archives, Washington, D.C.

NOTES

Introduction

1. Schlesinger, *The Age of Roosevelt*, 336; Owen, *Conservation Under F.D.R*, 4; Friedel, *Franklin D. Roosevelt* 1956, 224–225; Miller, *FDR: An Intimate History*, 315.

2. Owen, *Conservation Under F.D.R.*, 10; Bellush, *Franklin D. Roosevelt*, 90–91; Nixon, *Franklin D. Roosevelt and Conservation*, 210; Collingwood, "Forestry Aids the Unemployed," 550.

3. Friedel, *Franklin D. Roosevelt* 1956, 224–225; Friedel, *Franklin D. Roosevelt* 1990, 85.

4. Leuchtenburg, *Franklin D. Roosevelt and the New Deal*, 5. See also, Otis L. Graham, Jr., "Years of Crisis: America in Depression and War, 1933–1945," in William E. Leuchtenburg, ed., *The Unfinished Century: America Since 1900*, 359–368.

5. U.S. Congress, *An Act for the Relief of Unemployment Through the Performance of Useful Public Work and for Other Purposes*, Public Law 5, 73rd Congress, 1st Session, 1933, p. 1. See also Rosenman, *The Public Papers and Addresses of Franklin D. Roosevelt*, 2:80; Owen, *Conservation Under F.D.R.*, 13–14; Nixon, *Franklin D. Roosevelt and Conservation*, 143–144.

6. *Joint Hearings on Unemployment Relief*, S-598, 73rd Congress, 1st Session, 1933; K. Davis, *FDR: The New Deal Years*, 78; Simpson, *Franklin D. Roosevelt*, 1; Salmond, *The Civilian Conservation Corps*, 11–17; Johnson, "The Army and the Civilian Conservation Corps," 149, 153–155.

7. *Salt Lake Tribune*, April 9, 1933, cited by Baldridge, "Nine Years of Achievement," 11.

8. *Joint Hearings on Unemployment Relief*, S-598, 73rd Congress, 1st Session, 1933; Davis, *FDR: The New Deal Years*, 78; Simpson, *Franklin D. Roosevelt*, 1; Salmond, *The Civilian Conservation Corps*, 11–17; Johnson, "The Army and the Civilian Conservation Corps, 149, 153–155; U.S. Congress, Senate, S-598, 73rd Congress, 1st Session, March 28, 1933, *Congressional Record*, 77, pp. 929–936; March 31, 1933, *Congressional Record*, pp. 1012–1013.

9. Hanson, "The Civilian Conservation Corps in the Northern Rocky Mountains," 172.

10. Ibid., 173, 175.

11. U.S. Congress, *An Act for the Relief of Unemployment Through the Performance of Useful Public Work and for Other Purposes*, Public Law 5, 73rd Congress, 1st Session, 1933, 1; Salmond, *The Civilian Conservation Corps*, 23. Immediately prior to the passage of the original bill establishing the CCC, Representative Oscar DePriest of Illinois, the only African-American in Congress, persuaded representatives and senators to include an amendment prohibiting racial discrimination. In retrospect, although it is curious that such a provision was accepted into law, given the reality of race relations in the 1930s, what perhaps best explains the absence of any large scale opposition to the amendment is that congressional representatives were quite willing to make "exceptions," particularly when CCC appropriations would improve employment conditions back home.

12. Kifer, "The Negro under the New Deal," 79.

13. Rawick, "The New Deal and Youth," 138.

14. Salmond, *The Civilian Conservation Corps*, 99.

15. Johnson, "The Army, the Negro and the Civilian Conservation Corps," 87.

16. Gower, "The Struggle of Blacks for Leadership Positions in the Civilian Conservation Corps," 135.

17. Lacy, *The Soil Soldiers*, 78.

18. Merrill, *Roosevelt's Forest Army*, 55–56.

19. Hill, *In the Shadow of the Mountain*, xvii.

20. The following state accounts discuss various aspects of the New Deal relief agencies in California: Lavender, *California: A Bicentennial History;* Wheeler, *Black California: The History of African-Americans in the Golden State;* Caughey, *California: A Remarkable State's Life History;* Beck and Williams, *California: A History of the Golden State;* Goode, *California's Black Pioneers;* Lapp, *Afro-Americans in California*. The author examined a number of California community histories for a more detailed discussion of the New Deal agencies in general and the CCC in particular. None of the works discussed the CCC or African-Americans to any extent.

Chapter 1. Origin of the Civilian Conservation Corps in California

1. Webbink, "Unemployment in the United States, 1930–1940," 248–272.

2. Kearney, *Anna Eleanor Roosevelt*, 23.

3. Roosevelt, *This I Remember*, 162–163.

4. *New York Times*, 16 April 1935.

5. U.S. Congress, Senate, S-598, 73rd Congress, 1st Session, March 28, 1933; *Congressional Record*, 32, Pt. 1, pp. 929–936, March 31, 1933, pp. 1012–1013.

6. *The CCC: What It Is and What It Does*, 1–3; Salmond, *The Civilian Conservation*

Corps, 27–30; Harper, *The Administration of the Civilian Conservation Corps*, 30–32; Otis, *The Forest Service and the Civilian Conservation Corps*, 8; Steen, *The U.S. Forest Service: A History*, 214–215.

7. Matloff, *American Military History*, 413; Weigley, *History of the United States Army*, 402; Killigrew, *The Impact of the Great Depression on the Army*, 10–17.

8. Correspondence of the Department of War, *Official File 25*, "CCC," Franklin D. Roosevelt Library, Hyde Park, New York.

9. *The CCC: What It Is and What It Does*, 1–3; Salmond, *The Civilian Conservation Corps*, 27–30; Harper, *The Administration of the Civilian Conservation Corps*, 30–32.

10. Civilian Conservation Corps, *Administration Organization Chart*, 1933. Record Group 35, Records of the Civilian Conservation Corps, National Archives (hereafter cited as R.G. and NA), Washington, D.C.

11. Civilian Conservation Corps, *Final Report of the Director of the Civilian Conservation Corps*, 20.

12. Weiss, *Farewell to the Party of Lincoln*, 298; Nixon and Samuelson, "Estimates of Unemployment in the United States," 101–111.

13. U.S. Department of Commerce, Bureau of the Census, *Fifteenth Census of the United States, 1930: Population*, Vol. III, *The Labor Force*, Part I, p. 252; *Sixteenth Census of the United States, 1940: Population*, Vol. III, *Labor Force*, Part I, pp. 61–64; U.S. Federal Emergency Relief Administration, *Unemployment Relief Census*, October, 1933, Report No. 1, *United States Summary*, pp. 8, 94–112.

14. Melvin, *Youth—Millions Too Many?*, 77; Rawick, "The New Deal and Youth," 20; Kifer, "The Negro Under the New Deal," 80.

15. Melvin, *Youth—Millions Too Many?*" 88; Salmond, *A Southern Rebel*, 126.

16. Salmond, *A Southern Rebel*, 126; Cahn and Bary, *Welfare Activities of Federal, State, and Local Governments in California*, 33; *Fifteenth Census of the United States: 1930, Population*, Vol. 2, *General Report*, pp. 52, 69; U.S. Federal Emergency Relief Administration, *Unemployment Relief Census*, October 1933. According to William H. Mullins, the California Unemployment Commission, which traveled throughout the state, estimated that as early as 1932, 700,000 of the state's population were jobless. Mullins, *The Depression and the Urban West Coast*, 91–92.

17. *Fifteenth Census of the United States, 1930; California Compendium*, 15–17; Goode, *California's Black Pioneers*, 131.

18. U.S. Department of Commerce, *Fifteenth Census of the United States, 1930, Unemployment*, Vol. 1, Unemployment Returns by Classes, p. 143; DeGraff, "Negro Migration to Los Angeles, 1930–1950," 79; Lapp, *Afro-Americans in California*, 40.

19. *Annual Report of the National Urban League*, 1931, pp. 10–11, cited by Fisher, "A History of the Political and Social Development of the Black Community in California," 226.

20. Los Angeles *California Eagle*, July 27, 1934.

21. U.S. Department of Commerce, *Sixteenth Census of the United States, 1940: Population*, Vol. III, *Labor Force*, Part I, pp. 63–64; U.S. Federal Emergency Relief

Administration, *Unemployment Relief Census*, October 1933, Report No. 1, United States Summary, pp. 94–112; see also, Broussard, *Black San Francisco*, 114–115.

22. Dewey Anderson, California State Relief Administration, *Who Are On Relief in California?*, cited by Fisher, "A History of the Political and Social Development of the Black Community in California, 1850–1950," 227.

23. Weiss, *Farewell to the Parts of Lincoln*, 55; Salmond, *The Civilian Conservation Corps*, 27; Fishel, "The Negro in the New Deal Era," 115; Friedel, *Franklin D. Roosevelt* 1973, 266; Saalberg, "Roosevelt, Fechner, and the CCC," 172; Johnson, "The Army, the Negro and the Civilian Conservation Corps," 82.

24. Salmond, *The Civilian Conservation Corps*, 26–30; Merrill, *Roosevelt's Forest Army*, 8–11; "Enrollment Procedure, Civilian Conservation Corps," n.d., appended to *CCC Selection Division, General Correspondence*, California, 1933–1941, R.G. 35, NA, Washington, D.C.

25. Kifer, "The Negro under the New Deal," 4–13; Gower, "The Struggle of Blacks for Leadership Positions in the Civilian Conservation Corps," 125; Salmond, *The Civilian Conservation Corps*, 88–91; Saalberg, "Roosevelt, Fechner, and the CCC," 173.

26. Barrett G. Potter, for example, has noted that although the most overt racism in enrollment occurred in the South, New York, a "liberal" state, also had its "Negro Question." "Despite some minor opposition, the Corps was generally viewed with favor by New York's citizens although perhaps no single issue involving the agency was as great at that raised by the enrollment of black men." Potter, "The Civilian Conservation Corps and New York's "Negro Question during the Great Depression," 183–184.

27. CCC *Selection Division, General Correspondence*, "Narrative Report," April 1–20, California, 1938–1939, R.G. 35, NA, Washington, D.C. It is not at all clear why complaints in regard to selection came so late from California. Available sources of community and organizational complaints in the West did not surface until years after the Corps was established. Even in the state of Washington, it was not until 1938 that the African-American community protested discrimination in selection and enrollment in the state's CCC program; Gower, "The Struggle of Blacks for Leadership Positions in the Civilian Conservation Corps," 127.

28. Donald Wild, Selection Director, San Francisco County, to Dayton Jones, April 30, 1938, CCC *Selection Division, General Correspondence*, California, 1938–1939, R.G. 35, NA, Washington, D.C.

29. Jones to W. Persons, April 30, 1939, CCC *Selection Division, General Correspondence*, California, 1938–1939, R.G. 35, NA, Washington, D.C.

30. Robert Elliott, Selection Director, Imperial County, to Jones, April 14, 1938, CCC *Selection Division, General Correspondence*, California, 1938–1939, R.G. 35, NA, Washington, D.C.

31. Jones to Persons, March 28, 1941, CCC *Selection Division, General Correspondence*, California, 1933–1941, R.G. 35, NA, Washington, D.C.

32. Interview with Claude Pierce, Los Angeles, California, July 10, 1985; interview with Cleveland Jacobs, Los Angeles, California, July 9, 1985; interview with Willie Stovall, Los Angeles, California, July 9, 1985; interview with Herbert Walters, Long Beach, California, July 11, 1985.

33. Saalberg, "Roosevelt, Fechner, and the CCC," 185, 187; Potter, "The Civilian Conservation Corps in New York State," 184–185; Gower, "The Struggle of Blacks for Leadership Positions in the Civilian Conservation Corps," 129; Johnson, "The Army, the Negro and the Civilian Conservation Corps," 82; Sullivan, *Days of Hope*, 54. See also, Foner, *Blacks and the Military in American History*, 129–130; and Nalty, *Strength for the Fight*, 131. It is worth noting, parenthetically, that the appointment of commanders Slade and King came in an election year. No doubt the appointments were intended to attract African-American electoral support. After FDR's reelection, however, no additional appointments were made.

34. Information compiled from camp files, State of California, R.G. 35, NA, Washington, D.C.

35. *The Civilian Conservation Corps at Work,* 5, 7; Salmond, *The Civilian Conservation Corps,* 30–31; Freidel, *Franklin D. Roosevelt* 1973, 266.

36. Information compiled from camp files, *State of California,* R.G. 35, NA, Washington, D.C.; interview with Norman Moore, Los Angeles, California, July 10, 1985; Earl Parks, Burbank, California, to author, April 14, 1985; Donald Hobart, familiar with the administrative machinery of the CCC in California, commented that "the CCC used a very tricky technique for identifying Mexicans: W-1 for white enrollees and W-2 for Mexicans." However, this author's written sources revealed no such racial distinctions. Interview with Donald Hobart, Oakland, California, August 14, 1982. See Kenneth E. Hendrickson, "The Civilian Conservation Corps in the Southwestern States," in Whishenhunt, ed., *The Depression in the Southwest,* 20.

37. Parman, "The Indian and the Civilian Conservation Corps," 54; Weeks, "The Eastern Cherokee and the New Deal," in Dubofsky and Burwood, eds., *Women and Minorities during the Great Depression,* 154–170. See also Badger, *The New Deal,* 178–181; Merrill, *Roosevelt's Forest Army,* 31; Salmond, *The Civilian Conservation Corps,* 33–34; Parman, "The Indian and the Civilian Conservation Corps," 44, 54; Whisenhunt, *The Depression in the Southwest,* 20–21.

38. Parman, "The Indian and the Civilian Conservation Corps," 40.

39. Salmond, *The Civilian Conservation Corps,* 100.

40. Salmond, *The Civilian Conservation Corps,* 46; Merrill, *Roosevelt's Forest Army,* 42–54; Civilian Conservation Corps, "Narrative Reports of CCC Accomplishments," R.G. 35, NA, Washington, D.C.

41. Interview with Donald Hobart, Oakland, California, August 14, 1982; U.S. President, *Executive Order,* "Allocating Funds . . ."; *Federal Register* December 1, 1934, 6910B; *New York Times* May 10, 1933, July 15, 1934, April 14, 1935.

42. Donald Hobart, Sacramento, California, to author, August 11, 1982.

43. Albert McLoyd to Warren Scott, May 31, 1935, Civilian Conservation Corps, *Camp Inspection Reports*, California, 1933–1942, R.G. 35, NA, Washington, D.C. (hereafter cited as *Inspection Reports*, with specific camps cited where possible).

44. Melvin Brown to Warren Scott, June 1935, *Inspection Reports*, California, 1933–1942, R.G. 35, NA, Washington, D.C.; Robert Fechner to Jones, July 16, 1935, CCC *Selection Division, General Correspondence*, California, 1933–1941, R.G. 35, NA, Washington, D.C.

45. Johnson, "The Army, the Negro and the Civilian Conservation Corps," 84. James Humphrey informed me that he was also assigned to a mixed company in Idaho. Once there, the racial hostility among white enrollees was so overwhelming that he was forced to desert. James Humphrey in a letter to the author, May 11, 1985.

46. Salmond, "The Civilian Conservation Corps and the Negro," 79.

47. Jones to Persons, June 26, 1935, CCC *Selection Division, General Correspondence*, California, 1933–1941, R.G. 35, NA, Washington, D.C.

48. Ibid.

49. James F. Humphrey to author, May 11, 1985; interview with William Nelson, Los Angeles, California, July 9, 1985; interview with Norman Moore, July 10, 1985.

50. Herbert C. Walters to author, May 3, 1985; interview with Willie Stovall, July 9, 1985; James E. Humphrey to author, May 11, 1985; Earl Parks to author, June 27, 1985.

51. Algy F. Landry to author, June 23, 1985; interviews with William Nelson, July 9, 1985; Norman Moore, July 10, 1985; Willie Stovall, July 9, 1985.

52. Herbert Walters to author, May 3, 1985.

53. *Los Angeles California Eagle*, August 11, 1933.

54. Civilian Conservation Corps, *Reports and Correspondence of Camp Investigators*, "Reports of Investigation of Alleged Discrimination Against Colored Enrollees in 992 Company," *Civilian Conservation Corps*, California, n.d., R.G. 35, NA, Washington, D.C.; Charles H. Taylor, Assistant Director, CCC, to Walter Meadsay, Secretary to Senator William C. McAdoo (California), October 26, 1933.

55. *New York Times*, July 30, 1933.

56. Letter from E. M. Duncan to Colonel Louis Howe, July 27, 1933, *Official File 268*, "CCC," Franklin D. Roosevelt Library, Hyde Park, New York.

57. Wandall, "A Negro in the CCC," 25.

58. Walters to writer, May 3, 1985.

59. Interview with Norman Moore, July 10, 1985.

60. Interview with Willie Stovall, July 9, 1985; Algy Landry to author, June 23, 1985; interviews with Walter Jacobs, July 9, 1985; William Nelson, July 9, 1985.

61. Kifer, "The Negro under the New Deal," 18–19.

62. Letter from a concerned mother to Governor Henry H. Blood, April 26, 1935, cited by Baldridge, "Nine Years of Achievement, 338.

63. Fechner to Jones, July 16, 1935, *Correspondence of the Director, R.G. 35, NA, Washington, D.C.*

64. Weiss, *Farewell to the Party of Lincoln*, 54; John Saalberg (Roosevelt, Fechner, and the CCC," 175) also noted that when the issue of segregation in the CCC was presented to President Roosevelt, he refused to take any official action to stop it. See Gower, "The Struggle of Blacks for Leadership Positions in the Civilian Conservation Corps, " 126. See also, Watkins, *The Great Depression*, 219–223.
65. Fechner to Jones, July 16, 1935, *Correspondence of the Director, R.G. 35, NA, Washington, D.C.*
66. Los Angeles Inter-Denominational Ministers' Alliance to Franklin D. Roosevelt, November 20, 1935, CCC *Selection Division, General Correspondence*, California, 1933–1937, R.G. 35, NA, Washington, D.C.; James J. McEntee, Assistant Director to Los Angeles Inter-Denominational Ministers' Alliance, n.d., CCC *Selection Division, General Correspondence*, California, 1933–1937, R.G. 35, NA, Washington, D.C.
67. Congressman Thomas Ford to Fechner, August 20, 1935, CCC *Selection Division, General Correspondence*, "Negro Camps," California, 1933–1941, R.G. 35, NA, Washington, D.C.
68. Fechner to Thomas L. Griffith, Jr., President, Los Angeles Branch, National Association for the Advancement of Colored People, September 31, 1935, *Records of the National Association for the Advancement of Colored People, 1929–1941, Library of Congress, Washington, D.C.*
69. Griffith to Fechner, October 23, 1935, *Records of the NAACP, 1929–1941, Library of Congress, Washington, D.C.; Griffith to Marvin McIntyre, Assistant Secretary to the President, February 1, 1936, Records of the NAACP*, 1929–1941, Library of Congress, Washington, D.C.; Fechner to Griffith, November 7, 1935, *Records of the NAACP*, 1929–1941, Library of Congress, Washington, D.C.
70. Interviews with Walter Jacobs, July 9, 1985; Willie Stovall, July 9, 1985; Norman Moore, July 10, 1985; William Nelson, July 9, 1985; Donald Hobart, August 14, 1982.
71. CCC *Selection Division, Policy: Negro, General—Negro Question*, California, 1933–1942, R.G. 35, NA, Washington, D.C.

Chapter 2. African-American CCC Companies in California, 1935–1942

1. Civilian Conservation Corps, *Correspondence of the Division of Research and Statistics*, October 11, 1940, R.G. 35, NA, Washington, D.C.
2. Civilian Conservation Corps, *Work Projects Reports*, California, 1933–1942, R.G. 35, NA (hereafter cited as *Work Projects Reports*, with specific camps cited where possible).
3. Hobart to author, August 11, 1982.
4. Information from various camp files, *State of California*, R.G. 35, NA, Washington, D.C.
5. Hobart to author, August 11, 1982.

6. Interview with Willie Stovall, July 9, 1985; statement by Robert D'Hue, former enrollee, in a telephone interview, August 3, 1985.

7. *Inspection Reports,* Camp F-164, La Cienega, Elsinore, California, July 12, 1937, R.G. 35, NA, Washington, D.C.

8. Hobart to author, August 11, 1982.

9. *Inspection Reports,* Camp F-164, La Cienega, Elsinore, California, July 12, 1937, R.G. 35, NA, Washington, D.C.; Hobart to author, August 11, 1982. See Cutler, *The Public Landscape of the New Deal,* 59–61.

10. *Work Projects Reports,* 1933–1942, R.G. 35, NA, Washington, D.C.

11. *Work Projects Reports,* Camp NP-5, Kaweah, California, February 5, 1941, R.G. 35, NA, Washington, D.C.

12. *Work Projects Reports,* Camp F-160, Pine Valley, California, 1933–1942, R.G. 35, NA, Washington, D.C.

13. This information compiled from individual camp files, California, R.G. 35, NA, Washington, D.C.

14. *Inspection Reports,* Camp P-233, Jamul, California, October, 1936, R.G. 35, NA, Washington, D.C.; Hobart to author, August 11, 1982.

15. A. N. Langford to President Roosevelt, *Inspection Reports,* Camp P-233, Jamul, California, November 13, 1936, R.G. 35, NA, Washington, D.C.

16. *Inspection Report,* Camp P-233, Jamul, California, March 12, 1941, R.G. 35, NA, Washington, D.C.; *Inspection Reports,* 1933–1942, R.G. 35, NA, Washington, D.C.

17. *Work Projects Reports,* Camp P-295, Alta Loma, California, 1933–1936, R.G. 35, NA, Washington, D.C.

18. Hobart to author, August 11, 1982.

19. *Work Projects Reports,* Camp F-364, Wheeler Springs, California, 1937–1940, R.G. 35, NA, Washington, D.C.

20. "Enrollee" to Fechner, July 27, 1939, *Inspection Reports,* Camp Piedra Blanca, F-364, Wheeler Springs, California, R.G. 35, NA, Washington, D.C.

21. Charles Kenlan, assistant to the director to the adjutant general, January 6, 1940, *Inspection Reports,* Camp Piedra Blanca, F-364, Wheeler Springs, California, R.G. 35, NA, Washington, D.C.

22. *Inspection Report,* Camp F-157, Highland, California, August 8, 1941, R.G. 35, NA, Washington, D.C.; *Camp Inspection Reports,* 1933–1942, R.G. 35, NA, Washington, D.C.

23. Los Angeles District *News-Courier,* Civilian Conservation Corps, March 15, 1937 (hereafter cited as *News-Courier*); ibid., April 1, 1937.

24. CCC *Official Annual, Los Angeles, California, CCC District,* February 1, 1938, Ninth Corps, CCC, District Advertising Company, Baton Rouge, Louisiana, p. 89 (hereafter cited as *Official Annual*). According to John Ulrich, first vice president of the National Association of Civilian Conservation Corps Alumni (NACCCA), the publisher of the *Official Annual,* Direct Advertising Company, no longer has copies of the *Official Annuals* in its archives; they were given to the New York Public Library many years ago (John H. Ulrich to author, April 19, 1985). Incidentally, the

district *Annuals* were contracted by the War Department. Each company commanding officer reviewed the text. In most cases the writing was done by the camp educational adviser, then edited by the company commander. No materials went into the district *Annuals* that were not favorable or creditable to the posture of the staff. Interview with Donald Hobart, August 14, 1982. *Official Annual* supplied to the author through the courtesy of various former CCC enrollees.

25. Interview with Robert D'Hue, San Diego, California, August 3, 1985.
26. *News-Courier,* July 1, 1938.
27. Ibid.

Chapter 3. Camp Life: Education, Recreation, and Community Relations

1. *News-Courier,* September 15, 1936.
2. Interview with Norman Moore, Los Angeles, California, July 10, 1985.
3. *News-Courier,* September 15, 1936.
4. Lacy, *The Soil Soldiers,* 190.
5. *News-Courier,* May 25, 1936; April 1, 1937.
6. Hill, *The School in the Camps,* 9; Salmond, *The Civilian Conservation Corps,* 48.
7. Hill, *The School in the Camps,* 9.
8. Baldridge, "Nine Years of Achievement," 257; Hill, *The School in the Camps,* 21.
9. CCC *Administration Organizational Chart,* 1936, R.G. 35, NA, Washington, D.C.
10. Oxley, "CCC Educational Advisors," 282–284; *Inspection Reports,* 1933–1942, R.G. 35, NA, Washington, D.C.; statement by Robert D'Hue, former assistant educational adviser, in a telephone interview, August 3, 1985; Wright, "Negro Youth and the Federal Emergency Programs," 399; Brown, *The Civilian Conservation Corps and Colored Youth,* 5. Brown's text is a mimeographed brochure, "CCC Publications, CCC and the Negro," R.G. 35, NA, Washington, D.C.
11. Kifer, "The Negro under the New Deal," 54.
12. White and Maze, *Harold Ickes of the New Deal,* 118.
13. Gower, "The Struggle of Blacks for Leadership Positions in the Civilian Conservation Corps," 128.
14. Kifer, "The Negro under the New Deal," 56. Kifer reported that there were no African-American educational advisers on the West Coast prior to September 1935. However, my sources clearly indicate that California assigned its first African-American adviser in August 1935. *Inspection Reports,* Camp SP-7, Richmond, California, December 31, 1935, R.G. 35, NA, Washington, D.C.; *Official Annual,* 90; Salmond, *The Civilian Conservation Corps,* 190; Gower, "The Struggle of Blacks for Leadership Positions in the Civilian Conservation Corps," 128; Fishel, "The Negro in the New Deal Era," 115; Oxley, "Meeting Problems of Negro Enrollees," 115; Arthur W. Mitchell, U.S. Congress, "The New Deal and the Negro," 76th Congress, 3rd Session, March 18, 1940, *Congressional Record,* 86, p. 3021.

15. Gower, "The Struggle of Blacks for Leadership Positions in the Civilian Conservation Corps," 131–133; Kirby, *Black Americans in the Roosevelt Era,* 109; letter from President Roosevelt to Fechner, June 8, 1935, *Official File* 268, "CCC," Franklin D. Roosevelt Library, Hyde Park, New York. See Nordin, *The New Deal's Black Congressman,* 147.

16. Gower, "The Struggle of Blacks for Leadership Positions in the Civilian Conservation Corps," 132; letter from Fechner to President Roosevelt, June 6, 1935, *Official File 268,* "CCC," Franklin D. Roosevelt Library, Hyde Park, New York.

17. Gower, "The Struggle of Blacks for Leadership Positions in the Civilian Conservation Corps," 132. According the Dennis Nordin, shortly after Brown secured the publicity position, he was severely criticized by prominent black Washingtonians for his charges of racism leveled at President Roosevelt. Nordin, *The New Deal's Black Congressman,* 147.

18. *Inspection Reports,* Camp SP-7, Richmond, California, December 31, 1935, R.G. 35, NA, Washington, D.C.; *Official Annual,* p. 90; interview with Claude Pierce, Los Angeles, California, July 10, 1985.

19. Interview with Claude Pierce, July 10, 1985; *News-Courier,* July 1, 1938.

20. Interview with Claude Pierce, July 10, 1985.

21. Hobart to author, August 11, 1982.

22. *Fresno* (California) *Bee,* November 28, 1940.

23. Civilian Conservation Corps, *Camp Educational Reports,* Camp NP-5, Kaweah, California, February 5, 1941, R.G. 35, NA, Washington, D.C. (hereafter cited as *Camp Educational Reports,* with specific camps cited where possible).

24. *Camp Educational Reports,* Company 2925-C, Camp F-144, Wheeler Springs, California, March 2, 1937, R.G. 35, NA, Washington, D.C. Judging from correspondence from former enrollees, history courses were especially popular, since most corpsmen had limited knowledge of African-American history. Claude Pierce to author, June 19, 1985.

25. *Camp Educational Reports,* Company 2924-C, Camp SP-7, Jamul, California, March 12, 1941, R.G. 35, NA, Washington, D.C.

26. *Camp Educational Reports,* Company 2940-C, Camp SP-7, Richmond, California, December 31, 1935, R.G. 35, NA, Washington, D.C.

27. *Official Annual,* p. 95.

28. Ibid.; *News-Courier,* May 25, 1936.

29. *Camp Educational Reports,* Company 2940-C, Camp SP-7, Richmond, California, December 31, 1935, R.G. 35, NA, Washington, D.C.; *Camp Educational Reports,* Company 2923-C, Camp NP-5, Elsinore, California, July 12, 1937, R.G. 35, NA, Washington, D.C.; *Camp Educational Reports,* Company 2924-C, Camp P-233, Jamul, California, March 12, 1941, R.G. 35, NA, Washington, D.C.

30. Wright, "Negro Youth and the Federal Emergency Programs," 399; *Camp Educational Reports,* Company 2924-C, Camp NP-5, Elsinore, California, July 12, 1937, R.G. 35, NA, Washington, D.C.; *Camp Educational Reports,* Company 2924-C, Camp F-140, Pine Valley, California, July 12, 1937, R.G. 35, NA, Washington, D.C.;

interviews and letters to author; *Camp Educational Reports,* Company 2923-C, Camp NP-5, Elsinore, California, July 12, 1937, R.G. 35, NA, Washington, D.C.

31. Salmond, *The Civilian Conservation Corps,* 219; interviews and letters to author.

32. *News-Courier,* May 25, 1936; March 15, 1937; *Inspection Reports,* Camp NP-5, La Cienega, Elsinore, California, July 12, 1937, R.G. 35, NA, Washington, D.C.

33. Interview with Willie Stovall, in a telephone interview, April 27, 1985.

34. *Inspection Reports,* Camp F-240, Alta Loma, California, November 26, 1935, R.G. 35, NA, Washington, D.C.

35. Lacy, *The Soil Soldiers,* 178–184.

36. *News-Courier,* September 15, 1936.

37. M. J. Bowen to Fechner, December 31,1935, "Letter to Fechner," appended to *Inspection Report,* SP-7, Richmond, California, R.G. 35, NA, Washington, D.C.

38. *News-Courier,* July 1, 1938.

39. *Official Annual,* p. 89.

40. Interview with Robert D'Hue, San Diego, California, August 3, 1985.

41. *News-Courier,* July 1, 1938.

42. *Official Annual,* p. 91.

43. Interview with Claude Pierce, July 10, 1985.

44. Interview with Norman Moore, July 10, 1985; Willie Stovall, Los Angeles, California, July 9, 1985; statement by Robert D'Hue, former enrollee and assistant educational adviser, in a telephone interview, August 3, 1985.

45. Salmond, *The Civilian Conservation Corps,* 92.

46. Hobart to author, August 11, 1982; interview with Willie Stovall, July 9, 1985; information from Orlando Coons, in a telephone interview, August 17, 1985. I visited the Richmond police department for verification of this incident but was informed that all "minor" arrest records are destroyed after twenty years.

47. Interview with Donald Hobart, August 14, 1982.

48. *Official Annual,* p. 91.

49. Hobart to author, August 11, 1982.

50. Charles H. Taylor, assistant CCC director, to Representative George Burham (D-Calif.), May 15, 1936, CCC *Selection Division File, General Correspondence,* California, 1933–1937, R.G. 35, NA, Washington, D.C.; A. W. Stockman to James McEntee, March 23, 1936, CCC *Selection Division File, General Correspondence,* California, 1933–1937, R.G. 35, NA, Washington, D.C.

51. *Inspection Reports,* Camp SF-7, Elsinore, California, July 12, 1937, R.G. 35, NA, Washington, D.C.

52. *Supplementary Report,* August 8, 1935, "All Negro Company," appended to *Inspection Report,* F-164, Elsinore, California, July 13, 1935, R.G. 35, NA, Washington, D.C.; interview with Robert D'Hue, August 3, 1985; *San Diego* (California) *Union,* April 3, 1938.

53. Interview with Cleveland Jacobs, July 9, 1985; letters to author from James O. Whaley, San Diego, California, September 20, 1985; James E. Humphrey, Los Angeles, California, May 21, 1985.

54. Salmond, *The Civilian Conservation Corps*, 93.
55. *Inspection Reports*, Camp P-233, Jamul, California, March 12, 1941, R.G. 35, NA, Washington, D.C.; *Inspection Reports*, Camp F-164, Elsinore, California, December 12, 1935, R.G. 35, NA, Washington, D.C.; *Supplementary Report*, February 20, 1936, appended to *Inspection Reports*, F-240, Alta Loma, California, November 27, 1935, R.G. 35, NA, Washington, D.C.

Chapter 4. African-Americans in California's CCC

1. Merrill, *Roosevelt's Forest Army*, 112; Owen, *Conservation Under F.D.R.*, 137–138; interview with Donald Hobart, August 4, 1982; Sam S. Alfano, Goleta, California, to author, May 8, 1985. Mr. Alfano is recreation officer with the Department of Agriculture's Forest Service. See Otis, *The Forest Service and the Civilian Conservation Corps*, 41–42.
2. My conclusion that the economic impact of the CCC on the state was greater than other parts of the West is inconsistent with the findings of William H. Mullins, who argues that some California communities saw a bonanza in the addition of paid consumers entering the local economies. After the first groups arrived, CCC members had little impact on the economy of westerners. Mullins, *The Depression and the Urban West Coast*, 134.
3. Salmond, "The Negro in the Civilian Conservation Corps" 83, 87; Kirby, *Black Americans in the Roosevelt Era*, 49; Weiss, *Farewell to the Party of Lincoln*, 298.
4. Memorandum from Lt. Colonel E. M. Watson, Military Aide to the President, to Secretary Early, n.d., *Official File 268*, "CCC," Franklin D. Roosevelt Library, Hyde Park, New York.
5. Neal Guy to Persons, April 7, 1941, CCC *Selection Division, Policy: Negro, General*—"Negro Question," California, R.G. 35, NA, Washington, D.C.
6. Salmond, *A Southern Rebel*, 126; Williams, *Administration and Program Operation of the National Youth Administration*, 1.
7. *Relation of the Division of Negro Affairs to the General Program of the National Youth Administration* (Records of the Office of Negro Affairs, Record Group 119, National Archives, Washington, D.C.), cited by Poynton, "The Negro Division of the National Youth Administration," 58.
8. National Youth Administration, *Final Report, Division of Negro Affairs*, 1943, R.G. 119, National Archives, Washington, D.C. See also the Papers of Aubrey W. Williams, 1930–1959, Box 34, "Personal files," Franklin D. Roosevelt Library, Hyde Park, New York.
9. Poynton, "The Negro Division of the National Youth Administration," 58; Cole, "Black Youth in the National Youth Administration in California, 385–402.
10. Salmond, *A Southern Rebel*, 126.
11. U.S. Congress, House, 75th Congress, 3rd Session, March 14, 1938, *Congressional Record*, 83, Pt. 3, p. 3321. President Roosevelt's message to Congress recommending a study of the forest land problem.

12. Landry to author, June 23, 1985; interviews with William Nelson, Los Angeles, California, July 9, 1985; Willie Stovall, Los Angeles, California, July 9, 1985; Norman Moore, Los Angeles, California, July 10, 1985.

13. Humphrey to author, May 11, 1985; interviews with Walter Jacobs, Los Angeles, California, July 9, 1985; Willie Stovall, July 9, 1985; Cleveland Jacobs, Los Angeles, California, July 9, 1985; Landry to author, June 23, 1985. Other enrollees had similar comments.

14. Interviews with William Nelson, July 9, 1985; Claude Pierce, Los Angeles, California, July 10, 1985; Robert D'Hue, August 3, 1985.

15. Interviews with William Nelson, July 9, 1985; Claude Pierce, July 10, 1985; Robert D'Hue, August 3, 1985; Humphrey to author, May 11, 1985; interviews with Claude Pierce, July 10, 1985; Norman Moore, July 10, 1985.

16. Interviews with Claude Pierce, July 10, 1985; Walter Jacobs, July 9, 1985; William Nelson, July 9, 1985; Willie Stovall, July 9, 1985; Cleveland Jacobs, July 9, 1985.

17. Interview with Claude Pierce, July 10, 1985.

18. Interviews with Norman Moore, July 10, 1985; Robert D'Hue, August 3, 1985; Humphrey to author, May 11, 1985; Claude Pierce, July 10, 1985; Willie Stovall, July 9, 1985.

19. Interviews with Claude Pierce, July 10, 1985; William Nelson, July 9, 1985; Humphrey to author, May 11, 1985.

20. Humphrey to author, May 11, 1985; interviews with Claude Pierce, July 10, 1985; Willie Stovall, July 9, 1985; Norman Moore, July 10, 1985.

21. Interview with William Nelson, July 9, 1985.

22. Interviews with William Nelson, July 9, 1985; Walter Jacobs, July 9, 1985; Mrs. Algy Landry, Los Angeles, California, July 11, 1985; Norman Moore, July 10, 1985

23. Interviews with Claude Pierce, July 10, 1985; Robert D'Hue, August 3, 1985.

24. Information from Mrs. Offutt T. MacWilliams, in a telephone interview, August 3, 1985.

25. Interview with Willie Stovall, July 9, 1985; information from Orlando Coons, in a telephone interview, August 17, 1985.

26. Information from Mrs. Mildred Shores, in a telephone interview, July 9, 1985; interview with Norman Moore, July 10, 1985.

27. Interviews with William Nelson, July 9, 1985; Norman Moore, July 10, 1985; Claude Pierce, July 10, 1985; Mrs. Mildred Shores, July 9, 1985.

28. Salmond, "The New Deal and Youth," 144.

Chapter 5. Epilogue

1. Interviews with Cleveland Jacobs, July 9, 1985; Willie Stovall, July 9, 1985; Robert D'Hue, August 3, 1985; Landry to author, June 23, 1985; Humphrey to author, May 11, 1985.

2. *New York Times,* June 6, 1985. Congress in 1984 passed legislation that would have created an American Conservation Corps, which would have enrolled 70,000 to 100,000 unemployed men and women between the ages of fifteen and twenty-five to work on public lands. President Ronald Reagan vetoed that bill.

3. Susanne Levitsky, public information officer for the California Conservation Corps, to author, July 9, 1985.

4. Ibid; Bass, "A Reborn CCC Shapes Young Lives With an Old Idea," 57–58; *Los Angeles Herald,* October 14, 1984.

5. Wisconsin Conservation Corps, *Biennial Report,* (1995), p. 3; information from Marc Shupp, in a telephone interview, September 15, 1997. Mr. Shupp is a field support specialist for the Wisconsin Conservation Corps.

6. *New York Times,* September 19, 1982; Murray, *Losing Ground,* 223–227.

7. Levitsky to author, July 9, 1985.

8. Greenstein, "Losing Faith in 'Losing Ground,'" 12, 16–17.

9. Schwartz, *America's Hidden Success,* 39–40.

10. Levitan, "The Evolving Welfare System," 237–238.

11. U.S. Congress, House, *National And Community Service Trust Act of 1993,* Pub. L. 103–219, 103rd Cong., 1st Session, August 5, 1993, H.R. 2010, pp. 1–6; "National Service: Can Clinton Turn Concept Into Reality?" *Congressional Quarterly* 51 January 30, 1993: 218–221; "National and Community Service," 225–253.

12. Salmond, *The Civilian Conservation Corps,* 101; Lacy, *The Soil Soldiers,* 78.

13. Saalberg, "Roosevelt, Fechner, and the CCC," 173.

14. Sitkoff, *A New Deal for Blacks,* 329.

15. Lacy, *The Soil Soldiers,* 209.

BIBLIOGRAPHY

Reports, Government Publications, Documents, and Papers

Annual Report of the National Urban League, 1931. Washington, D.C.: Library of Congress, 1931.

Brown, Edgar G. *The Civilian Conservation Corps and Colored Youth.* Washington, D.C.: Office of the Director, 1940.

The CCC: What It Is and What It Does. Washington, D.C.: Government Printing Office, 1939.

Civilian Conservation Corps. *Administration Organization Chart.* National Archives and Records Service, Record Group 35, Washington, D.C., 1933.

———. *Camp Educational Reports,* California, 1933–1942. National Archives and Records Service, Record Group No. 35, Washington, D.C.

———. *Camp Inspection Reports,* California, 1933–1942. National Archives and Records Service, Record Group No. 35, Washington, D.C.

———. *Correspondence of the Chief Liaison Officer,* 1938–1942. National Archives and Records Service, Record Group No. 35, Washington, D.C.

———. *Correspondence of the Director,* 1933–1942. National Archives and Records Service, Record Group No. 35, Washington, D.C.

———. *Correspondence of the Division of Research and Statistics,* 1933–1942. National Archives and Records Service. Record Group No. 35, Washington, D.C.

———. *Division of Planning and Public Relations. General Correspondence,* 1933–1942, "N."

———. *Final Report of the Director of the Civilian Conservation Corps,* 1933–1942. Washington, D.C.: Government Printing Office, 1942.

———. *Official Annual, Los Angeles, California CCC District.* Baton Rouge, La.: Direct Advertising Company, 1938.

———. *Report of the Director of the Civilian Conservation Corps,* 1933–1942. Washington, D.C.: Government Printing Office, 1942.

———. *Reports and Correspondence of Camp Investigators,* California, 1933–1942. National Archives and Records Service, Record Group No. 35, Washington, D.C.

———. *Selection Division, Policy: Negro, General—Negro Question* (Alabama–Wyoming). National Archives and Records Service, Record Group No. 35, Washington, D.C.

————. *Selection Division State File, General Correspondence,* California, 1933–1937. National Archives and Records Service, Record Group No. 35, Washington, D.C.

————. *Standards of Eligibility and Selection for Junior Enrollees.* Washington, D.C.: Government Printing Office, June 15, 1939.

————. *Work Projects Reports,* California, 1933–1942. National Archives and Records Service, Record Group No. 35, Washington, D.C.

The Civilian Conservation Corps at Work. Washington, D.C.: Federal Security Agency, 1940.

Congressional Record. 1933–1942. Washington, D.C.

Helms, Douglas. *Readings in the History of the Soil Conservation Service.* Washington, D.C.: USDA Soil Conservation Service, 1992.

Matloff, Maurice. *American Military History.* Washington, D.C.: Office of the Chief of Military History United States Army, 1973.

Merriam, Governor Frank F. Papers, 1934–1938. Bancroft Library, University of California, Berkeley, California.

Otis, Alison T. *The Forest Service and the Civilian Conservation Corps: 1933–42.* Washington, D.C.: USDA Forest Service, 1986.

Paige, John C. *The Civilian Conservation Corps and the National Park Service, 1933–1942: An Administrative History.* Washington, D.C.: Government Printing Office, 1985.

Records of the Division of Negro Affairs, 1935–1943. National Youth Administration, Record Group No. 119, National Archives, Washington, D.C.

Records of the National Association for the Advancement of Colored People. Washington, D.C.: Library of Congress, 1929–1941.

Roosevelt, Franklin D., Papers. *Official File 25,* "War Department," Franklin D. Roosevelt Library, Hyde Park, New York, 1933–1945.

————. *Official File 93,* "Colored Matters," Franklin D. Roosevelt Library, Hyde Park, New York, 1928–1945.

————. *Official File 177,* "Conservation Matters," Franklin D. Roosevelt Library, Hyde Park, New York, 1933–1945.

————. *Official File 268,* "Civilian Conservation Corps," Franklin D. Roosevelt Library, Hyde Park, New York, 1928–1945.

————. *Official File 268,* "Participation of the War Department in the Civilian Conservation Corps, April, 1933–March 31, 1935," Franklin D. Roosevelt Library, Hyde Park, New York, 1933–1945.

————. *Official File 324,* "Army Posts and Reservations," Franklin D. Roosevelt Library, Hyde Park, New York, 1933–1945.

————. *President's Personal File 30,* "Colored Matters," Franklin D. Roosevelt Library, Hyde Park, New York, 1933–1945.

————. *President's Personal File 7082,* "Edgar G. Brown," Franklin D. Roosevelt Library, Hyde Park, New York, 1933–1945.

Selected Documents from the Papers of Eleanor Roosevelt and Aubrey Williams and the National Youth Administration Correspondence, 1935–1942, in the Franklin D. Roosevelt Library, Hyde Park, New York.

U.S. Department of Commerce, Bureau of the Census. *Census of the United States: California Compendium*, 1930–1940.

———. *Census of the United States: Population*, 1930–1940.

U.S. Department of the Interior, National Park Service. *The CCC and Its Contribution to a Nation-wide State Park Recreational Program*. Washington, D.C.: Government Printing Office, 1937.

U.S. Federal Emergency Relief Administration. *Unemployment Relief Census*, October 1933. Washington, D.C.

U.S. House of Representatives. *National and Community Service Trust Act of 1993*. H.R. 2010, 103rd Congress, 1st session, 1993.

U.S. President. Executive Order. "Allocating Funds from the Appropriation to Meet the Emergency and Necessity for Relief in Stricken Agricultural Areas." *Federal Register*, December 1, 1934, 6910-B.

Williams, Aubrey. *Administration and Program Operation of the National Youth Administration*. Washington, D.C.: United States Government Printing Office, 1937.

———. *Personal Files*, 1930–1959. Franklin D. Roosevelt Library, Hyde Park, New York.

Wisconsin Conservation Corps, 1993–95. *Biennial Report*. Madison: Wisconsin Conservation Corps, 1995.

Books and Articles

Armstrong, Frank H. "Civilian Conservation Corps Revival." *Journal of Forestry* 57 (April 1971):224–225.

Arrington, Leonard. "The New Deal in the West: A Preliminary Statistical Inquiry." *Pacific Historical Review* 38 (August 1969):311–316.

Badger, Anthony J. *The New Deal: The Depression Years, 1933–1940*. New York: Noonday Press, 1989.

Bagnell, Beth. *Oakland: The Story of a City*. Novato, Calif.: Presidio Press, 1982.

Bailin, Michael A., and Natalie Jaffee. *The State Youth Initiatives Project: The California Conservation Corps: A Case Study*. Philadelphia: Public/Private Ventures, 1982.

Bass, Thomas A. "A Reborn CCC Shapes Young Lives with an Old Idea." *Smithsonian* 14 (April 1938):57–66.

Beck, Warren A., and David A. Williams. *California: A History of the Golden State*. New York: Doubleday, 1972.

Bellush, Bernard E. *Franklin D. Roosevelt: A Governor of New York*. New York: Columbia University Press, 1955.

Braeman, John, and Robert Brody. *The New Deal: The National Level*. Columbus: Ohio State University Press, 1975.

———. *The New Deal: The State and Local Level*. Columbus: Ohio State University Press, 1975.

Bremer, William W. "Along the 'American Way.' The New Deal's Work Relief Program for the Unemployed." *The Journal of American History* 62 (December 1975):636–652.

Broussard, Albert S. *Black San Francisco: The Struggle for Racial Equality in the West, 1900–1954.* Lawrence: University Press of Kansas, 1993.

Bunche, Ralph J. *The Political Status of the Negro in the Age of FDR.* Chicago: University of Chicago Press, 1973.

Burke, Robert E. *Olson's New Deal for California.* Berkeley: University of California Press, 1953.

Burns, James MacGregor. *Roosevelt: The Lion and the Fox.* New York: Harcourt, Brace and World, 1956.

Cahn, Francis, and Valeska Bary. *Welfare Activities of Federal, State, and Local Governments in California.* Berkeley: University of California Press, 1936.

Carr, Harry. *Los Angeles: City of Dreams.* New York: D. Appleton-Century, 1935.

Case, Walter H. *History of Long Beach And Vicinity.* New York: Arno Press, 1974.

Caughey, John, and Laree Caughey. *Los Angeles: Biography of a City.* Berkeley: University of California Press, 1976.

Caughey, John W. *California: A Remarkable State's Life History.* Englewood Cliffs, N.J.: Prentice-Hall, 1970.

Cohen, Sol. "Remember the CCC?" *Phi Delta Kappa* 79 (March 1968):369–372.

Cole, Olen, Jr. "African-American Youth in the Program of the Civilian Conservation Corps in California, 1933–1942: An Ambivalent Legacy." *Forest & Conservation History* 35 (July 1991):121–127.

————. "Black Youth in the National Youth Administration in California, 1935–1943." *Southern California Quarterly* 73 (Winter 1991): 385–402.

Cole, Susan D. *Richmond: Windows to the Past.* Richmond, Calif: Wildcat Canyon Books, 1980.

Collingwood, G. H. "Forestry Aids the Unemployed," *American Forests* 38 (October 1932):550.

Conkin, Paul K. *The New Deal.* Arlington Heights, Ill.: Harlan Davidson, 1992.

Cutler, Phoebe. *The Public Landscape of the New Deal.* New Haven, Conn.: Yale University Press, 1985.

Daniels, Henry D. *Pioneer Urbanites: A Social and Cultural History of Black San Francisco.* Philadelphia: Temple University Press, 1980.

Davis, John P. "A Black Inventory of the New Deal." *The Crisis* 5 (May 1935):141–154.

Davis, Kenneth S. *FDR: Into the Storm, 1937–1940: A History.* New York: Random House, 1993.

————. *FDR: The Beckoning of Destiny, 1882–1928: A History.* New York: G. P. Putnam's Sons, 1971.

————. *FDR: The New Deal Years, 1933–1937: A History.* New York: Random House, 1986.

Davis, Kingsley. *Youth in the Depression.* Chicago: University of Chicago Press, 1935.

Davis, Maxine. *The Lost Generation: A Portrait of American Youth Today.* New York: Macmillan, 1936.

Dubofsky, Melvyn, and Stephen Burwood, eds. *Women and Minorities during the Great Depression.* New York: Garland Publishing, 1990.

Eden, Robert, ed. *The New Deal and Its Legacy: Critique and Reappraisal.* New York: Greenwood Press, 1989.

"Eight Years of the CCC." *Newsweek.*(April 14, 1941):23.

Ellis, Edward R. *A Nation in Torment: The Great American Depression, 1929–1939.* New York: Coward-McCann, 1970.

Elman, Richard M. *Ill-at-Ease in Compton.* New York: Pantheon Books, 1967.

Ervin, John R. *The Participation of the Negro in the Community of Los Angeles.* San Francisco: R & E Research Associates, 1973.

Fishel, Leslie. "The Negro in the New Deal Era." *Wisconsin Magazine of History* 43 (Winter 1964):111–126.

Foner, Jack D. *Blacks and the Military in American History: A New Deal Perspective.* New York: Praeger, 1974.

Forbes, Jack D. *Afro-Americans in the Far West: A Handbook for Educators.* Berkeley: Far West Laboratory for Education Research and Development, 1969.

———. *Native Americans of California and Nevada.* Healdsburg, Calif.: Naturegraph Publishers, 1969.

France, Edward E. *Some Aspects of the Migration of the Negro to the San Francisco Bay Area since 1940.* San Francisco: R and E Research Associates, 1962.

Franklin, John Hope, and Alfred A. Moss, Jr. *From Slavery to Freedom: A History of African Americans.* New York: McGraw-Hill, 1994.

Fraser, Steve, and Gary Gerstle, eds. *The Rise and Fall of the New Deal Order, 1930–1980.* Princeton, N.J.: Princeton University Press, 1990.

Frazier, E. Franklin. "The Status of the Negro in American Social Order." *Journal of Negro Education* 4 (July 1935):293–307.

Friedel, Frank B. *Franklin D. Roosevelt.* 4 Vols. Boston: Little, Brown, 1956.

———. *Franklin D. Roosevelt: A Rendezvous with Destiny.* Boston: Little, Brown, 1990.

Ganoe, William A. *The History of the United States Army.* New York: D. Appleton-Century, 1942.

Garden City Women's Club: History of Black Americans in Santa Clara Valley. San Jose, Calif.: Garden City Women's Club, n.d.

Goode, Kenneth. *California's Black Pioneers.* Santa Barbara, Calif.: McNally and Loftin, 1974.

Goodman, Marian. *San Mateo County: Its Story.* Redwood City, Calif.: Goodman Publishing Company, 1967.

Gower, Calvin W. "The Struggle of Blacks for Leadership Positions in the Civilian Conservation Corps: 1933–1942." *Journal of Negro History* 2 (April 1976):123–135.

Graham, Otis, ed. *The New Deal: The Critical Issues.* Boston: Little, Brown, 1971.

Graham, Otis, and Meghan Robinson Wander, eds. *Franklin D. Roosevelt: His Life and Times.* Boston: G. K. Hall, 1985.

Greenstein, Robert. "Losing Faith in 'Losing Ground'." *New Republic* 192 (March 25, 1985):12–17.

Hagan, William T. *American Indians.* Chicago: University of Chicago Press, 1979.

Hansen, Gladys, ed. *San Francisco: The Bay and Its Cities.* New York: Hastings House, 1973.

Harper, Charles. *The Administration of the Civilian Conservation Corps.* Clarksburg, W.Va.: Clarksburg Publishers, 1939.

Hausler, Donald. "Blacks in Early Oakland." Oakland, Calif., Public Library: Unpublished monograph, 1986.

Henri, Florette. *Black Migration: Movement North, 1900–1920*. Garden City, N.Y.: Anchor Books, 1976.

Hill, Edwin G. *In the Shadow of the Mountain: The Spirit of the CCC*. Pullman: Washington State University Press, 1990.

Hill, Frank E. *The School in the Camps: The Educational Program of the Civilian Conservation Corps*. New York: American Association for Adult Education, 1935.

Hinkel, Edgar, and William E. McCann, eds. *History of Oakland, 1852–1938*. Oakland, Calif.: Oakland Public Library, 1939.

History of Alameda County California. Oakland, Calif.: Holmes Book Company, 1969.

History of Contra Costa County. Oakland, Calif.: Brooks-Sterling, 1974.

Hoffman, Abraham. *Unwanted Mexican Americans in the Great Depression: Repatriation Pressures, 1929–1939*. Tucson: University of Arizona Press, 1974.

Holland, Kenneth, and Frank E. Hill. *Youth in the CCC*. Washington, D.C.: American Council on Education, 1942.

Holland, Reid A. "Life in Oklahoma's Civilian Conservation Corps." *The Chronicles of Oklahoma* 68 (Summer 1970):224–234.

Hoyt, Ray. *We Can Take It: A Short History of the CCC*. New York: Americana Book Company, 1935.

Humphreys, Hubert. "In a Sense Experimental: The Civilian Conservation Corps in Louisiana." *Louisiana History* 5 (Winter 1964):345–367.

Johnson, Charles W. "The Army and the Civilian Conservation Corps, 1933–1942." *Prologue* 4 (Fall 1972):139–155.

———. "The Army, the Negro and the Civilian Conservation Corps: 1933–1942." *Military Affairs* 3 (October 1972):82–87.

Kearney, James R. *Anna Eleanor Roosevelt: The Evolution of A Reformer*. Boston: Houghton Mifflin, 1968.

Killigrew, John W. *The Impact of the Great Depression on the Army*. New York: Garland Publishing, 1979.

Kinnaird, Lawrence. *History of the Greater San Francisco Bay Area*. 3 Vols. New York: Lewis Historical Publications, 1966.

Kirby, John B. *Black Americans in the Roosevelt Era: Liberalism and Race*. Knoxville: University of Tennessee Press, 1980.

———."The Roosevelt Administration and Blacks: An Ambivalent Legacy." *Twentieth Century America: Recent Interpretations*. 2nd ed., Barton T. Bernstein and Allen J. Matusow, eds. New York: Harcourt Brace Jovanovich, 1972.

Korstain, Clarence F. *Forestry on Private Lands in the United States*. Durham, N.C.: Duke University Press, 1944.

Lacy, Leslie A. *The Soil Soldiers: The Civilian Conservation Corps in the Great Depression*. Radnor, Pa.: Chilton, 1976.

Lapp, Rudolph. *Afro-Americans in California*. San Francisco: Boyd and Fraser, 1979.

Lash, Joseph P. *Dealers and Dreamers: A New Look at the New Deal*. Doubleday, 1988.

Lavender, David. *California: A Bicentennial History.* New York: W. W. Norton, 1976.

Leuchtenburg, William. *Franklin D. Roosevelt and the New Deal, 1932–1940.* New York: Harper and Row, 1963.

———, ed. *The Unfinished Century: America since 1900.* New York: Little, Brown, 1973.

Levitan, Sar A. "The Evolving Welfare System." *Society* (January/February 1986) 237–42.

Lewis, Betty. *Watsonville: Memories that Linger.* Fresno, Calif.: Valley Publishers, 1976.

Lowitt, Richard. *One-Third of a Nation: Lorena Hickok Reports on the Great Depression.* Urbana: University of Illinois Press, 1981.

———. *The New Deal and the West.* Bloomington: Indiana University Press, 1984.

McEntee, James J. *Now They Are Men: The Story of the CCC.* Washington, D.C.: National Home Library Foundation, 1940.

Melvin, Bruce L. *Youth—Millions Too Many? A Search for Youth's Place in America.* New York: Association Press, 1940.

Merrill, Perry H. *Roosevelt's Forest Army: A History of the Civilian Conservation Corps.* Montpelier, Vt.: Perry H. Merrill, 1981.

Miller, Nathan. *FDR: An Intimate History.* Garden City, N.Y.: Doubleday, 1983.

Morgan, Ted. *FDR: A Bibliography.* New York: Simon and Schuster, 1985.

Mullins, William H. *The Depression and the Urban West Coast, 1929–1933.* Bloomington: Indiana University Press, 1991.

Murray, Charles. *Losing Ground: American Social Policy, 1950–1980.* New York: Basic Books, 1984.

Myrdal, Gunnar. *An American Dilemma: The Negro Problem and Modern Democracy.* New York: Harper and Row, 1944.

Nalty, Bernard C. *Strength for the Fight: A History of Black Americans in the Military.* New York: Free Press, 1986.

Nash, Gerald D. *The American West Transformed.* Bloomington: Indiana University Press, 1985.

"National and Community Service." *Congressional Digest* 72 (October 1993):225–253.

"National Service: Can Clinton Turn Concept into Reality." *Congressional Quarterly* 51 (January 30, 1993): 218–21.

Nishki, Dennis. *Life During the Great Depression.* San Diego, Calif.: Lucent Books, 1998.

Nixon, Edgar, ed. *Franklin D. Roosevelt and Conservation, 1911–1934.* Washington: National Archives and Records Service and the Franklin D. Roosevelt Library, 1957.

Nixon, Russell A., and Paul A. Samuelson. "Estimates of Unemployment in the United States." *Review of Economic Statistics* 22 (August 1940):101–111.

Noble, John Wesley. *Its Name Was M.U.D.: A History, East Bay Municipal District.* N.p., 1970.

Nordin, Dennis S. *The New Deal's Black Congressman: A Life of Arthur Wergs Mitchell.* Columbia: University of Missouri Press, 1997.

"Old, New CCCs Changed Many Lives." *Sacramento Bee* (March 27, 1983): A3–4.

Oliver, Alfred C., Jr., and Harold M. Dudley. *This New America: The Spirit of the Civilian Conservation Corps.* New York: Longman, Green, 1937.

Owen, A. L. Riesch. *Conservation Under F.D.R.* New York: Praeger, 1983.

Oxley, Howard W. "CCC Educational Advisors." *School Life* 25 (June 1940):283–284.

———. "Meeting Problems of Negro Enrollees." *School Life* 22 (January 1933):145–155.

Parman, Donald L. "The Indian and the Civilian Conservation Corps." *Pacific Historical Review* 40 (February 1971):39–56.

Patterson, James R. "The New Deal in the West." *Pacific Historical Review* 39 (August 1969):317–327.

Pettitt, George A. *Berkeley: The Town and Gown of It.* Berkeley, Calif.: Howell-North Books, 1973.

Potter, Barrett G. "The Civilian Conservation Corps and New York's "Negro Question": A Case Study in Federal-State Race Relations during the Great Depression." *Afro-Americans in New York Life and History* 1 (July 1977):183–199.

Reiman, Richard A. *The New Deal & American Youth: Ideas & Ideals in a Depression Decade.* Athens: University of Georgia Press, 1992.

Rogin, Michael, and John Shover. *Political Change in California: Critical Elections and Social Movements, 1890–1966.* Westport, Conn.: Greenwood Publishing, 1970.

Roosevelt, Eleanor. *This I Remember.* New York: Harper and Brothers, 1949.

Rosenman, Samuel, I., ed. *The Public Papers and Addresses of Franklin D. Roosevelt.* New York: Random House, 1938–50.

Rutledge, Archibald. "The Negro and the New Deal." *South Atlantic Quarterly* 39 (July 1940):281–289.

Salmond, John A. *The Civilian Conservation Corps, 1933–1942: The New Deal Case Study.* Durham, N.C.: Duke University Press, 1967.

———."The Civilian Conservation Corps and the Negro." *The Journal of American History* 52 (June 1965):73–88.

———. "The New Deal and Youth," in G. A. Ward and P. S. O'Connor, eds., *Essays Presented to William P. Morrell.* Dunedin, Australia: Otago University Press, 1973, pp. 141–163.

———. *A Southern Rebel: The Life and Times of Aubrey Williams, 1890–1965.* Chapel Hill: University of North Carolina Press, 1983.

Schlesinger, Arthur, Jr. *The Age of Roosevelt: The Coming of the New Deal.* Boston: Houghton Mifflin, 1959.

Schwartz, John E. *America's Hidden Success: A Reassessment of Twenty Years of Public Policy.* New York: W. W. Norton, 1983.

Sheehey, Katherine S. "Conserving Corps Memories." *Westways* 77 (April 1985):36–39.

Simpson, Michael. *Franklin D. Roosevelt.* New York: B. Blackwell, 1989.

Sitkoff, Harvard. *A New Deal for Blacks: The Emergence of Civil Rights as a National Issue.* Vol. 1, *The Depression Decade.* New York: Oxford University Press, 1978.

———, ed. *Fifty Years Later: The New Deal Evaluated.* New York: Knopf, 1985.

Sloane, Howard N., and Lucille L. Sloane. *The Goodyear Guide to State Parks.* New York: Crown Publishers, 1967.

Starr, Kevin. *Endangered Dreams: The Great Depression in California.* New York: Oxford University Press, 1996.

Steen, Harold K. *The U.S. Forest Service: A History.* Seattle: University of Washington Press, 1976.

Steindl, Frank G. *Monetary Interpretations of the Great Depression.* Ann Arbor: University of Michigan Press, 1995.

Sterner, Richard. *The Negro's Share: A Study of Income, Consumption, Housing and Public Assistance.* New York: Harper and Brothers, 1943.

Sternsher, Bernard, ed. *The Negro in Depression and War: Prelude to Revolution 1930–1945.* Chicago: Quadrangle Books, 1969.

Stuart, Reginald R. *San Leandro: A History.* San Leandro, Calif.: First Methodist Church, 1951.

Sullivan, Patricia. *Days of Hope: Race and Democracy in the New Deal Era.* Chapel Hill: University of North Carolina Press, 1996.

Swain, Donald C. *Federal Conservation Policy.* Berkeley: University of California Press, 1963.

Symon, Charles A. *We Can Do It! A History of the Civilian Conservation Corps in Michigan—1933–1942.* Escanaba, Mich.: Richards Printing, 1983.

Terkel, Studs. *Hard Times: An Oral History of the Great Depression.* New York: Avon, 1971.

Wandall, Luther C. "A Negro in the CCC." *The Crisis* 42 (August 1935):244–254.

Watkins, T. H. *The Great Depression: America in the 1930s.* New York: Little, Brown, 1993.

Weaver, Robert C. "The New Deal and the Negro. A Look at the Facts." *Opportunity: Journal of Negro Life* 13 (July 1935):200–203.

Webbink, Paul. "Unemployment in the United States, 1930–1940," *Papers and Proceedings of the American Economic Association* 30 (February 1941):248–272.

Wecter, Dixon. *The Age of the Great Depression: 1929–1941.* New York: Macmillan, 1948.

Weeks, Charles J. "The Eastern Cherokee and the New Deal." *North Carolina Historical Review* 53 (Summer 1976):303–319.

Weigley, Russell F. *History of the United States Army.* New York: Macmillan, 1967.

Weiss, Nancy J. *Farewell to the Party of Lincoln: Black Politics in the Age of FDR.* Princeton, N.J.: Princeton University Press, 1983.

Wheeler, B. Gordon. *Black California: The History of African-Americans in the Golden State.* New York: Hippocrene Books, 1993.

Whisenhunt, Donald W., ed. *The Depression in the Southwest.* Port Washington, N.Y.: Kennikat Press, 1980.

White, Graham, and John Maze. *Harold Ickes of the New Deal.* Cambridge: Harvard University Press, 1985.

Whitnah, Joseph C. *A History of Richmond California.* Richmond, Calif.: Richmond Chamber of Commerce, 1944.

Wolters, Raymond. *Negroes and the Great Depression: The Problem of Economic Recovery.* Westport, Conn.: Greenwood Publishing, 1970.

Wright, Marian T. "Negro Youth and the Federal Emergency Programs: CCC and NYA." *The Journal of Negro Education* 9 (July 1940): 397–407.

Wye, Christopher G. "The New Deal and the Negro Community: Toward a Broader Conceptualization." *The Journal of American History* 59 (December 1972):621–639.

Zuckman, Jill. "The President's Call to Serve Is Clear but Undefined." *Congressional Quarterly* 51 (January 1993):218–221.

Interviews and Correspondence

The following individuals have supplied the writer with information either by means of interviews or correspondence. Most are former enrollees. Some have been kind enough to provide photographs, CCC newspapers, and other unpublished materials, as well as their personal recollections of the Corps and its work.

Alfano, Sam S. Goleta, Calif., letter, May 8, 1985.
Coons, Orlando. San Diego, Calif., interview, August 17, 1985.
D'Hue, Robert. San Diego, Calif., interview, August 3, 1985.
Graham, Lorenz. Claremont, Calif., letter, May 1, 1985.
Henley, Charles E. Manassas, Va., letter, July 15, 1982.
Hobart, Donald. Sacramento, Calif., letter, August 11, 1982.
———. Oakland, Calif., interview, August 14, 1985.
Humphrey, James. Los Angeles, Calif., letter, May 11, 1985.
Jacobs, Cleveland. Los Angeles, Calif., interview, July 9, 1985.
Jacobs, Walter. Los Angeles, Calif., interview, July 9, 1985.
Johnson, Joseph P. Los Angeles, Calif., letter, June 23, 1985.
Landry, Algy. Los Angeles, Calif., letter, June 23, 1985.
Landry, Mrs. Algy. Los Angeles, Calif., interview, July 11, 1985.
Larson, Kenneth L. Los Angeles, Calif., letter, April 15, 1985.
Levitsky, Susanne. Sacramento, Calif., letter, July 9, 1985.
MacWilliams, Mrs. Offutt. San Diego, Calif., interview, August 3, 1985.
Moore, Norman. Los Angeles, Calif., interview, July 10, 1985.
Nelson, William. Los Angeles, Calif., interview, July 9, 1985.
Parks, Earl. Burbank, Calif., letters, April 14, June 27, 1985.
Pierce, Claude. Los Angeles, Calif., letter, June 19, 1985, and interview, July 10, 1985.
Salmond, John A. Chapel Hill, N.C., interview, September 9, 1982, and letter, October 21, 1982.
Shores, Mrs. Mildred. Los Angeles, Calif., interview, July 9, 1985.
Shupp, Marc. Madison, Wis., interview, September 15, 1997.
Stovall, Willie. Los Angeles, Calif., telephone interview, April 27, 1985, and personal interview, July 9, 1985.
Ulrich, John H. Carpinteria, Calif., letter, April 9, 1985.
Walters, Herbert. Long Beach, Calif., interview, July 11, 1985, and letters, April 14, May 3, 1985.
Whaley, James O. San Diego, Calif., interview, August 20, 1985, and letter, September 18, 1985.
Yellen, Ben. Brawley, Calif., letter, April 8, 1985.

Dissertations and Theses

Baldridge, Kenneth W. "Nine Years of Achievement: The Civilian Conservation Corps in Utah." Ph.D. dissertation, Brigham Young University, 1971.

deGraff, Lawrence B. "Negro Migration to Los Angeles, 1930–1950." Unpublished Ph.D. dissertation, University of California, Los Angeles, 1962.

Fisher, James A. "A History of the Political and Social Development of the Black Community in California, 1850–1950." Ph.D. dissertation, State University of New York at Stony Brook, 1972.

Hanson, James A. "The Civilian Conservation Corps in the Northern Rocky Mountains." Unpublished Ph.D. dissertation, University of Wyoming, 1973.

Kifer, Allen. "The Negro under the New Deal." Ph.D. dissertation, University of Wisconsin, 1961.

Maskin, Melvin R. "Black Education and the New Deal: The Urban Experience." Ph.D. dissertation, New York University, 1973.

Maxwell, John C. "Social Welfare Attitudes in California during the Thirties." Ph.D. dissertation, University of California, Los Angeles, 1971.

Potter, Barrett G. "The Civilian Conservation Corps in New York State: Its Social and Political Impact, 1933–1942." Ph.D. dissertation, State University of New York at Buffalo, 1973.

Poynton, Susan M. "The Negro Division of the National Youth Administration, 1935–1943." M.A. thesis, La Trobe University, 1975.

Rawick, George P. "The New Deal and Youth: The CCC, NYA, and the American Youth Congress." Ph.D. dissertation, University of Wisconsin, 1957.

Saalberg, John J. "Roosevelt, Fechner, and the CCC: A Study in Executive Leadership." Ph.D. dissertation, Cornell University, 1962.

Newspapers

Christian Science Monitor. May 30, 1985.
Fresno Bee. 1933–1940.
Los Angeles *California Eagle.* 1933–1934.
Los Angeles District *News-Courier* (CCC). 1936–1938.
New York Times. 1933–1982.
Salt Lake City Tribune. April 9, 1933.
San Diego Union. 1933–1940.
Stockton Record. September 27, 1982.

INDEX